DRY GROUND INTO WATERSPRINGS

by
Armon Dawson

Published by
WYCLIFFE BIBLE TRANSLATORS, INC.
Huntington Beach, California

About the Cover

Mt. Juarez taken from the author's favorite cactus forest at the edge of the town of Tasquillo, ten miles north of Ixmiquilpan. Juarez was the George Washington of Mexico. In this photograph, his head is lying with his chin closest to the tall organ cactus.

The title was chosen from Psalms 107, verses 35-37.

International Standard Book Number — 0-918544-09-2

Printed and Published by Wimmer Brothers Books
P.O. Box 540
Memphis, TN 38101

To Vera my wife,
and to my three daughters
Lillian, Evelyn, and Katharine

FOREWORD

I first met Armon and Vera Dawson in Mexico City in 1959. It was at that time that they became acquainted with the Otomi people and the work in progress among them. I was able to observe personally the way God stirred their hearts with the conviction of the importance of providing people with God's message of love and also assisting them in practical ways. Our friendship grew as the Dawsons came again and again to visit the work of Wycliffe among the Otomi and in other places in Mexico.

I have known few people, either missionaries or laymen, who have shouldered the burden of proclaiming God's Word to those who have never had it as squarely as Armon and Vera Dawson. Their commitment is very deep, as will be observed by reading their story in the following pages.

Dry Ground into Watersprings shows how lay-people can get involved in missionary service. The Dawsons got involved and have been of tremendous service in the cause of Bible translation. I believe others can match their example, and I hope their story will serve as a challenge for many others to do so. We pray this may be the result.

Benjamin F. Elson, Secretary
Wycliffe Bible Translators, Inc.

PREFACE

A steady stream of tourists daily leaves our land and flocks into every foreign country and onto almost every island. Most tourists are good ambassadors, but again, some are not. Missionaries living and working in these countries number in the tens of thousands. A tourist can be a blessing to a missionary or he can be a nuisance.

I have been in a mixed group of tourists and missionaries, participating in and listening to conversations on various subjects being discussed. I have been embarrassed to hear tourists relate to each other how many pairs of fifty-dollar shoes they own. Is this visitor courtesy, when the Lord has called these missionaries to work among some people who have **no** shoes, and there are those of His called servants who may have only one pair?

Or a tourist is in a village in the company of a missionary, and they encounter an appealing, energetic shoeshine boy. Wishing to help the boy, he gets a shoeshine. When he asks the boy the price of his services, the lad replies, "One peso." But instead of giving him the required amount, a peso or one and a half, the tourist pays him a U.S. quarter or even a half-dollar. The boy's eyes light up, his smile broadens, and he advertises his good fortune as soon as possible. In no time at all, the tourist and the missionary are surrounded by outstretched hands, with voices calling pitifully, "Dimey, dimey."

The tourist has hurt the missionary in two ways. In all probability, he is of the same nationality as the missionary, and the latter will be expected to overpay for every service rendered him from now on. Also the visitor has encouraged a gang of beggars that the missionary must live and cope with after the tourist has gone.

Sometimes a tourist is drawn to a handsome, polite, bright-eyed boy living in a primitive village. He thinks to himself, "Wouldn't it be a good idea to send that boy out where he can get a good education, perhaps become a doctor who will come back and practice medicine among his own people? If he could be educated, I would do this village a great service. I'll do it."

Through the overtures of well-intentioned tourists, some boys have been sent out to receive an education, with the anticipation that they will return to serve the villages where they spent their childhood. A few such have returned to become blessings to their people, but the great majority have experienced a change when they tasted the affluent life, saw the bright lights, heard the melodic sounds and smelled the delightful odors. Only rarely does one go back to help his own people.

Missionaries, therefore, can never be sure how tourist brainstorms will work out because situations frequently develop that get out of control. I can see why missionaries take a dim view of every suggested project until they are assured that it is God-inspired. It is my conviction that every project a tourist proposes should have the complete approval of the workers serving the people who will be affected.

Our venture with the agriculture project among the Otomi began and ended happily. This was because every step was taken only after consultation with and full approval of the Director of the Mexico Branch of Wycliffe Bible Translators and all the missionaries working among the Otomi.

This book is not an account of what we have done for the Otomi, but a sincere personal account of what the Otomi people have done for us. They have taught us what can be accomplished with a little, as when Jesus fed so many with the loaves and fishes.

It took the Otomi believers to show us that many of our ideas had been wrong, simply because we had the cart before the horse. We needed to reverse our priorities.

Another reason for narrating these experiences is to say that if we, a very ordinary pair of farm people, can get ourselves so delightfully involved, no doubt you can too. No one likes to be compelled, but it is a great joy to get involved.

—Armon Dawson

ACKNOWLEDGMENT

Writing books is not among our family traits. I have not studied journalism, nor even been in school since 1922. As this project took shape, I have needed all the help and encouragement I could get. I must therefore express my appreciation, acknowledge the encouragement, and thank the persons who proofread my manuscript. They were honest enough to offer criticism, corrections, and helpful suggestions, and expressed confidence enough to keep me at it. The Otomi leaders knew that this story was being undertaken, and they carefully supplied bits of information in the interest of accuracy.

No one has attempted to keep a record of the many hours of precious time which Don and Isabel Sinclair, Nancy Lanier, Harwood and Pat Hess, Patricia (Cowan) Beller, and later Richie Anderson, gave to us — the many miles driven and many hours sacrificed interpreting English to Otomi and vice versa, and we are grateful for every one. Since Don and Isabel lived on Colony Hill, they were easiest to contact and most often available, until it seemed at times we were imposing too much on their generous natures. Whenever we mentioned any need, they always made us feel that our wishes were of the utmost importance. We are forever indebted to the Sinclairs and their jeep station wagon.

Don decided to teach me how to speak Otomi, after I began to get involved in a land project. It seemed a good idea, and he had the best of intentions. His principal problem was that he could not get me to settle down in one place long enough. He gave up on me when I finally suggested that it would probably be easier to teach the Otomi to speak English. I did learn to say two Otomi words in sixteen years — an embarrassing lack of achievement. Otomi is a nasal language, and my nasal equipment just wasn't made for it.

The language barrier between people of different tongues is high and wide, and there is no easy way to surmount it. According to the most accurate report available, gathered by many sources, the languages confounded at Babel have multiplied considerably. The latest statistics show that as of January 1, 1975, there are 5,687 spoken languages in the world. The accuracy of my information in this narrative is the result of data accumulated by professionally trained linguist friends.

We are grateful to the Lord for bringing the Reverend and Mrs. Robert Collett into our lives at exactly the right time, with the right amount of persuasion to influence us. At their urging, we became acquainted with Wycliffe Bible Translators and later Bill

8

and Marj Nyman hosted our visit to the Mezquital Valley and to Colony Hill. There we met and came to know a number of Otomi believers.

These are the people who have changed our lives. No one missionary has influenced us more than Miss Ethel Wallis, however — by her writings, her fellowship and conversation, and her several speaking engagements from Indianapolis platforms. In March, 1962, as she rode with us in our car toward Taxco, south of Mexico City, she told us that a faithful prayer partner of many years had recently died. Would we be willing to take his place? We marveled that one so talented, well-known — a successful translator, author, speaker, and educator — would ask us to replace her veteran prayer partner of many years. Nevertheless, our prayers have followed her through thick and thin, wherever the Lord has led her, during the years since that day. Because the Otomi people were those whom God had laid on her heart and for whom she served as a member of the translation team, is doubtless one of the reasons I became willing to put our experiences in the form of a book.

I hold the greatest respect for Wycliffe Bible Translators and its far-reaching ministry. A technique, a timetable, and a finished task — isn't that what it's all about? And today we find we have the same love and admiration for Wycliffe as that which was kindled when Bob Collett first took us to their headquarters. The Otomi-and-Wycliffe package from God to us contained precious gifts that we needed and cherished.

In fact, I would have no story to tell it if had not been for Wycliffe Bible Translators. Dr. Benjamin Elson, Director of Wycliffe's Mexico Branch, became our example of Christian administration and leadership. The high esteem that remains in our hearts had its effect in imparting to me the necessary boldness to express and share my feelings toward pioneer missions. We thank God for the encouragement of the Elsons.

When I completed the first rough draft of my manuscript, I handed it to a Florida neighbor, a retired English teacher, to read. I am grateful for her reading of it, but more appreciative of what she had to say. Although she did remark that it needed more done to it than she had time to do, she also commented, "It is interesting — and it sounds like you, all right."

I rewrote parts of it and then submitted it to my family. Each read it and furnished me with a written list of corrections, criticisms, and encouragements that, added together, put me on my toes. It fanned into flame a story that had been smoldering in my heart for a couple of years. I accepted the challenge and set it down on paper. I hope it still sounds "like me, all right."

I especially thank God for the invaluable assistance of understanding and cooperative editors, particularly Ethel Wallis in Dallas and Elizabeth Stevens in Huntington Beach. They have worked with me separately, and later as a team, in preparing and finishing my manuscript for public acceptance.

I never realized what a feeling comes over one when he hands a manuscript to others to read, for a true appraisal of his thoughts, beliefs, actions, reactions, shortcomings, failures, faith, and ideals. In so doing he has bared his soul and stands defenseless and exposed. So I send forth this chronicle of the deepest experience of my life, with the hope that it may bless and motivate as God shall choose.

CONTENTS

GLOSSARY

Important — The letter a is always pronounced as a in father — accent marks are important.

Abrazo - a-bra'-so — a Mexican hug or embrace
Celedonia - Sell-eh-doan-ya — the Pastor's wife
Chapultepec - Cha-pool-ta-peck — the first field we bought
Chiapas - Chee-a'-pas — a state in southern Mexico
Chichicastenango - Chee-chee-kas'-ten-ango — a famous witchcraft center in Guatemala
Costumbre - Coast-oom'-bray — a Guatemalan witchdoctor's ritual
El Maye - El My'-yea — a town west of our land
Ixmiquilpan - Ishma-keel'-pan — the name of the town, an important Otomi center where Colony Hill is located
Juarez - Wha'-res — the famous mountain on the book cover picture
Mezquital - Mess'-key-tal — the name of the valley
Mitla - Meet'-la — where another workshop center is, near the city of Oaxaca
Morales - Mor-al'-ace — the land where gamio linguistics center is located
Oaxaca - Wa-ha'-ka — a city in the state of Oaxaca 350 miles south of Mexico City
Otomi - Oh-toe-me' — the tribal people
Péso - pay'-so — the Mexican dollar, worth .08¢ in 1959, now worth .04½¢
Quetzlcoatl - Ketz-all-coatl' — Toltec feathered serpent god
Tasquillo - Task-key'-oh — the village from which cover picture is taken, also where Teke and Pat Hess lived
Teofilo - Tea-oh'-feel-oh — the beliver who watched his son slain because of his new faith
Teotihuecan - Tay-oh-tee-wa-cahn — an area north of Mexico City where the famous pyramids are located
Tetzu - Tet-soo' — the village where the Ethel Wallis house is located
Tito - Tea'-toe — Venancio's cousin and perhaps his first convert
Venancio - either Ben-an'-sea-o or Ven-an'-sea-o — the pastor and Otomi spiritual leader
Zimapan - Seam'-ah-pan — a town on the northern edge of the valley

CHAPTER ONE
THE MEZQUITAL VALLEY

As I sit here with my wife and daughters on this warm, spring night in Mexico, I think of the chilly morning we left behind in Indianapolis yesterday. In this audience of more than five thousand people, ninety percent of them Otomi, I sense we are witnessing the culmination of a work of divine providence in this place.

The event is the dedication ceremony of the Templo Sinai new church on Colony Hill at Ixmiquilpan, Hidalgo, Mexico, located at kilometer 159, one hundred miles north of Mexico City. Colony Hill is near the Pan American Highway which cuts through the town. This area is known as the Mezquital Valley. It is the heart of Otomi country, and thus these people are known as the Otomi of the Mezquital.

The mesquite, a spiny tree or shrub, once covered northern Mexico, but because of lack of authoritative supervision, the trees have suffered at the hands of hoards of people who desperately needed firewood and material for charcoal marketable at villages and towns. Thus, today the land is noticeably barren.

The Mezquital Valley lies high in the Sierra Madre mountain range at altitudes varying from 4400-6000 feet. Colony Hill at 5500 feet is 500 feet higher than Denver, Colorado. The Valley extends from the town of Actopan on the south to Zimapan in the north, and from Progresso in the west to Deca and Defai on the east. It is populated by more than one hundred thousand Otomi, most of whom are monolingual in their mother tongue and faithful to their unique cultural pattern. Perhaps 15% speak Spanish.

Probably one of the dominant factors that has prohibited and discouraged improvement in the mode of life of these people is the lack of water in any form — rain, rivers, creeks, lakes, or wells. In the summer of 1959, I noted an article in a news magazine which stated that the Mexican Government had driven test wells more then 3,000 feet deep, in several locations in the Mezquital without finding water. Since the Tula River is the only stream which penetrates a relatively few miles in and out of the west side of the dry, dusty valley, the lack of water and the endless days of hot sunshine the year round, combined with a perpetual warm wind, are not conducive to a supply of sufficient foodstuff.

However, in the last ten years the center of the valley has experienced considerable relief, as conduits and canals have been hewn in the stone valley floor. Now water is carried by gravity from the mountain springs around the peripheral rim, high enough to give the water sufficient fall. The Mexican Government has also constructed cement cisterns in villages located along the Pan American Highway and hauls water to them periodically in tanker trucks.

In the 1950's, it was commonly said that the Otomi of the Mezquital were the poorest of Mexico's peoples, as a result of the absence of rainfall and the consequent lack of food supply. Where there was any moisture, the land produced like a Garden of Eden, but this only occurred where there was irrigation. When the only moisture was furnished by the dew of night, the lone green growing thing was cactus. Consequently, hunger and poverty prevailed. My observation has been that the well-being of the Otomi had been in direct ratio to the streams of water diverted out of the Tula River and the mountains to provide irrigation to an arid and thirsty land.

These improvements have been made at considerable expense; therefore the first such blessings have been enjoyed only by those who could afford this affluence. These benefits did not include many Otomi, but additional food supply did come into the hands of those Otomi who worked as laborers in the fields of wealthy Mexican landowners for a half-dollar or less per day. Perhaps the Otomi may still be considered the poorest and most undernourished of the peoples of Mexico, but in my judgment their improved condition is gradually removing them from the critical list.

CHAPTER TWO
THOSE AMAZING OTOMI

What does all this have to do with the dedication of a new church of believing brethren on Colony Hill in Ixmiquilpan? What does all this have to do with my belief that this church is a result of divine providence? I didn't set out to tell only the economic problems of a group of people. There is far more to the actual story. It is found in transformed lives, the result of the translated Word of God. That, to me, is where the excitement is.

It may not seem to you that the dedication of a new church building seating 5000 people is enough to get excited about. Many people in the States worship in churches larger than that. But when you consider that the population of Ixmiquilpan is only

3000 people, half of whom are Mexicans, the dedication of this Otomi church crowns an achievement that calls for a red-letter day. Then to look around in all directions and find every seat occupied, including some 600 in the balcony, the aisles filled with people standing, while a dozen or so peer in at each open window — one must admit that this is extraordinary. An element is present here which evidences more than hard work and good management.

I estimate there may be 250-300 North Americans scattered through this audience, most of them Wycliffe Bible Translators and similar groups who work in Mexico with some 140 languages other than Spanish. Then there are a score or more of Stateside people like my family attending for a variety of reasons. I suppose nearly a hundred Mexicans are present, including some Government officials from Mexico City seated near the front. Of course, officials of Ixmiquilpan and of neighboring towns and villages have been invited. The great majority of this audience, however, are Otomi believers of the Mezquital Valley. The entire service will probably last two hours, and ever word spoken, prayer made and hymn sung, will issue in Otomi — not English or Spanish.

The best way to find out where all these people came from and why is to listen to the welcoming remarks of the pastor, Venancio Hernandez. Venancio is the spiritual leader whose horizon was high enough to see and include every nook and cranny of this rugged and difficult terrain. He has an "upper room" in his home, situated perhaps two hundred feet away. Alone in this room, he has sought and received the will of God for the leadership of the Colony Church, from its humble beginnings until now when it is great. Very few ideas have come out of that upper room on a trial-and-error basis. Plans emerged from that sacred upper room with God's approval, or they did not come out.

Since I do not understand much Spanish and only speak it in the vernacular of the marketplace, and with only two words in my Otomi vocabulary — "Good morning," and "Good afternoon" — how am I to know what Venancio is saying? I would not if it were not for the Wycliffe linguist sitting between me and my wife, whispering key sentences and phrases into our ears, keeping a thread of thought running through our minds. This, pieced together with facts that we have already known, makes it clear enough so I can tell you the profound statement he is making.

"In this audience of believers, sitting, standing, and peering in every door and window, are representatives of some one hundred plus congregations of Otomi believers having been influenced and established as kindred churches to this church that

15

Excellent picture of Venancio Hernandez, spiritual leader and pastor of Colony Hill Church.

Photograph by Hugh Stevens

we are dedicating here today. They came from far and near in the Mezquital Valley and extending north as far as Tamazunchale, overlapping Huastecan country. We are of common bond and spirit, and we welcome everyone of you to share this day of victory and rejoicing."

That is about what I expected Venancio to say in his welcoming remarks this morning, because I heard him say similar things on April 25, 1971, on this very site when the Otomi New Testament was dedicated. You see, this is not our first trip to Mexico and to the town of Ixmiquilpan. This is my twenty-second trip and my wife's eighteenth visit to Mexico since January, 1959.

It was late one Saturday afternoon in the early months of 1959 that I observed Venancio, the pastor, and Tito Espinosa, the assistant pastor, as they preached and taught a small group of sincere and attentive Otomi men, using a Spanish Bible but speaking to them in their native tongue. Later I discovered that this group of learners scattered in every direction early on Sunday mornings, walking over rough paths, riding bicycles when possible, hitchhiking with a passing truck when available — using any means, to get to little congregations who waited for them to arrive. Their purpose in making these tortuous journeys was to preach in Otomi the sermon they had learned the previous evening.

One day I said to Venancio, "I'm interested in these men who go out to pastor churches and congregations located away from this one on Colony Hill. How many of these young Timothys are there? How many congregations do they represent?" And Venancio answered, "There are now eight, and some of them preach to more than one congregation."

Much planning and hard work went into preparation for the day of dedication of the Otomi New Testament on April 25th, 1971. I think in that preparation they also had in mind this dedication today. When they prepared that site, they were also getting ready the site where this magnificent church would be built. The ground was leveled and packed, after a steep bank had been removed where the church foundation was to be. A rough network of ropes and wire was suspended by poles to make a ceiling to support tree branches, slats and greenery, providing partial shade from the burning sun for those seated on chairs and benches underneath. Barbecue pits had been dug, and enough goats were prepared so that, along with hundreds of tortillas and cases of soda pop, there was abundant food to invite all who attended the ceremonies to eat together afterward. It was such a blessed and triumphant day that the church chose to make it their day of remembrance which they would celebrate each year.

The platform built for the 1971 ceremony, with a pulpit made of stacked Bibles, was located in just about the same place as where the platform and pulpit stand in this new church. And Venancio stands today at nearly the same spot where he stood then, when he remarked, "In this audience of more than two thousand people, gathered to hear and witness the dedication of the blessed Word of God, in the New Testament given to us in our own language, are representatives of 64 congregations of believers, having been influenced and established as kindred churches to the one where we worship in this Colony not far from here. It is so greatly overcrowded that only a small portion of the people who came from here and there can find entrance."

Did you notice the rate of growth, from a dozen congregations in 1959 to 64 in 1971? In March, 1973, Venancio told me in Mexico City that the number had by that time increased to 70 congregations. In mid-December, 1974, he wrote me a letter saying that the crowds of people from 80 congregations converging upon the Colony church for special occasions, so overwhelmed the existing facilities that they were compelled to meet in the walls of this unfinished new church before it had a roof. They stood from wall to wall. Today, Venancio acknowledged at least five thousand people, probably some 4,500 of them Otomi from 100-plus separate and established congregations. I find the best words to exclaim are, "Those amazing Otomi!"

Church facilities on Colony Hill in 1959 seating 150 people have grown to facilities in 1978 seating 5,000, while 12 kindred underling churches in 1959 have multiplied until in 1978 some 100-plus such groups thrive — an extraordinary rate of growth. Where have you ever seen it equalled? How has your own church fared in that length of time? You can see why I am sometimes tempted to call this new church a miracle church.

My wife and I have heard true and exciting stories of the Chamula, the Totonac, the Tzeltal, the Zapotec, the Mazatec, the Aztec and others in Mexico. We know stories of thousands of believers, native leaders, congregations, Bible schools, New Testament dedications, spiritual growth — coming from many places around the world. But the reason I call the people of the Mezquital Valley "those amazing Otomi," is because they are our first love, and we know of no other such consistent Christian testimony.

A view of the new church of the Otomi, Teofilo stands before the church.
Take note that the roof is self-supporting with no interior posts to obstruct
the view in the sanctuary.

Venancio stands at the base of the front of the new church.

CHAPTER THREE
THE PLAN AND TIMETABLE

On that day in 1971 when the New Testament was being dedicated on this level, unimproved spot, there was hanging from a post at the left of the speaker's platform a set of blueprints. These prints were enlarged to perhaps four feet by seven feet, hung high on the post so that they could be seen, whether one was sitting or standing. These were the plans for this new church now finished and being dedicated. Venancio pointed them out to the audience, as he referred to the urgent needs of the fast-growing Otomi church and its influence expanding in every direction. In that reassuring voice of authority that he possesses, he quietly remarked, "We need this new church as soon as possible, and we must begin its construction at once. In fact, the long, level place where you are seated is wide enough for the entire foundation on which to build this church."

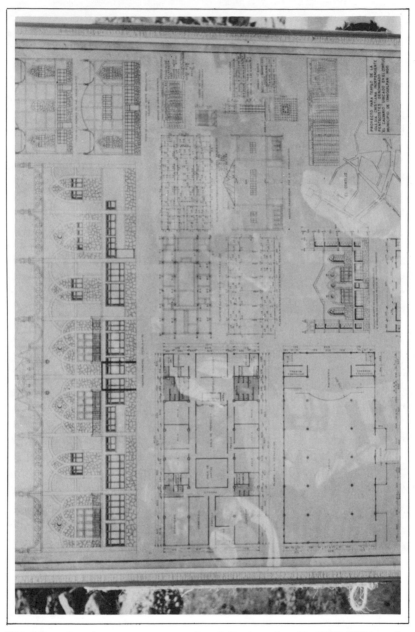

This blueprint plan was announced and displayed on April 25, 1971, at the dedication of the New Testament, on the site for the new church. Already built, the new church seats 5,000 people and cost more than a million pesos, yet it is completely paid for.

That same evening, in his home, I examined the blueprints which had just been brought. I complimented Venancio on the great step of faith he was proposing. I felt it was the greatest I had ever seen anywhere. I asked God's blessing upon the planning and the work that would have to be done.

Before leaving, I asked Venancio what he estimated the new church would cost. He replied thoughtfully, "Six hundred thousand pesos" ($48,000 U.S.). I then asked, "How much do you have on hand now?" He replied without hesitation, "Seventy-five thousand pesos." Then I asked him the question that logically came next. "Where will you get the rest?" His immediate reply was, "The Lord will give it to us." That I never doubted for one minute. So this new church is no surprise to me. Venancio is never certain about things as important as this until he gets his answers in his "upper room," and he never speaks about them until he is certain they are from the Lord "Whose he is and Whom he serves." The truth is that this church cost considerably more than Venancio's estimate. But it is completely paid for, and the Lord did give the remainder to them.

My wife and I have learned many valuable lessons from these Otomi friends during the last sixteen years. Since we did not anticipate any part of our early relationship, and since we do not believe in luck, we can only acknowledge that God had some new experiences in store for us. To bring about our spiritual growth, he used a strange chain of circumstances to get us to the right place at the right time, for all of which we are eternally grateful. This whole Otomi experience has been amazing. Such supernatural linking together of circumstances doesn't happen every day. We trust it will prove a blessing to you, as we recap what happened.

CHAPTER FOUR
A BACKGROUND AND PREPARATION

I was born the only child of a central Indiana farm couple. My parents were strict and zealous in keeping the Lord's Day and in church attendance. They went to church in both fair and foul weather, driving a horse and buggy seven miles each way. I have been told that they took me to church when I was three weeks old. In other words, I have been attending church for more than seventy years.

My childhood, adolescence, and young manhood were normal and routine for a farm boy — full of advantages and joys and the usual amount of growing pains, ever learning but never quite fast enough. My devout mother would have been pleased if I had become a minister, I am sure, and she would have been completely overjoyed if I had turned out to be a missionary. My practical dad was pleased that I became a farmer, his junior partner for more than thirty years.

I became a Christian in 1916, and I can truthfully say that I kept my ear to the ground, wondering if I would hear a call from the Lord into the ministry — or better yet, to become a missionary. But I did not hear anything, so I became reconciled to stay home and strive to be always my pastor's righthand man. I served in every office of my denominational church year after year for thirty-seven years.

There is an old adage that says, "We are fast becoming that which we are to be." I suppose a good way to interpret that is to observe and analyze a large snowball that has been rolled up to become the body of a snowman. In the process of being rolled, the snow picks up things besides snow, like twigs, leaves, feathers, pebbles, dead weeds, and string. A person my age realizes that in the process of rolling, he has picked up a lot of stuff besides snow — not all of it good or all of it bad. Some of it we would like to eliminate and some we are glad we've acquired.

Grandparents seem to have a way of tucking some good influences into the lives of growing boys and girls. I was pretty well exposed to the lifestyle and philosophy of one of my grandfathers, and I'm sure he gave me a few traits and challenges. In 1908 my maternal grandmother died, and soon afterward my grandfather closed his home and for the rest of his life spent his winters in Florida and alternated his summers in the homes of his son and two daughters. There are three things that I can remember that he said and did while he was living in my parents' home. I can't recall the exact circumstances, but one day he remarked to me, "Sonny, a person has just so many words to say, and when he gets them said, he's got to die. I must tell you, I think you are using up your words too fast, and I think you're going to run out too soon."

At another time he commented on the son of a prominent couple, a boy who had gotten into trouble, that "It is only three generations between the pulpit and the penitentiary."

The most delightful remembrance was of riding with him in horse-and-buggy days, as he went to the store for Mom or the blacksmith shop or gristmill for Dad. Dozens of times as we jogged along I have listened to him humming, "Amazing Grace." It

23

isn't strange that "Amazing Grace" was my mother's favorite song, and it is mine also. It was one of the good things that I got rolled up in my snowball, about which I am glad.

In 1925 I married my highschool sweetheart, Vera. My parents had built a new home and moved a mile west of the farm that summer, so Vera and I set up housekeeping in the farm home where I had lived with my parents for twenty-one years. Vera belonged to another denominational church and attended there until our marriage. Together we decided that she should bring her church membership to my church, about four miles south of where we lived. It was a good decision, because we established a Christian home and were soon involved as a couple in the affairs and activities of a church made up mostly of rural people and farmers who worked hard on the farms and in the church.

By 1934 we had three daughters, three and four years apart. When one reached five or six years of age, she found herself responsible for certain farm chores, and became a part of the team. In a couple of years she would surrender her chores and teach them to the next younger, so that she herself might tackle bigger and more important tasks. As this went on for many years, through grade school, high school, college, and a succession of summer vacations, we became an efficient farm family.

All during these good growing years, our Christian lives needed considerable chiseling and buffing with abrasives as a refining process.

It was easy — too easy — to neglect our spiritual needs. It was not difficult on the farm to become too busy and weary to read the Bible and pray with the family, other than on Sunday. Like too many Americans, we were preoccupied in providing food for our bodies and neglectful of food for our spiritual lives. We needed to learn costly lessons, especially I, the husband and father as head of the household. One of these lessons from the Lord's hand proved to be a buffing with plenty of abrasion — and it was painful.

As long as I can remember, I have liked a Jersey dairy cow. Every place that we went I kept a lookout for Jersey cattle. I could see a Jersey cow at a farther distance than anything else, in anyone's pasture field or woods. At the State Fair the Jersey cattle were the fairest of them all. When I was nineteen years old, Dad and I bought a truckload of Tennessee Jersey heifers that were about one year old. By the time I was married, these heifers were producing milk. This was my first dairy herd and it was my pride and joy. Talk about togetherness! These heifers brought me and my wife together both morning and evening about 5 a.m. and 5 p.m., each milking five by hand. This was our routine for a couple of years until I bought an electric milker. In a year or two I placed my herd in the Indiana State Dairy Herd Improvement Association, known as DHIA. Under supervised testing, the first year they earned a silver medal awarded at Purdue University. They were awarded another silver medal the second year. Eight months inside the third year they qualified for a silver medal. Their production remained high enough, however, that a gold medal was possible at the end of the third year — in fact, it seemed imminent. But before the year ended, my world caved in.

Shortly after midnight on November 3, 1930, the Lord decided to teach me an important lesson, and to impress it, He chose to make it severe. We were roused suddenly out of deep sleep by loud pounding and yelling at the front door, when a neighbor boy screamed out, "Armon! Armon! Your barn is burning down!" My heart died within me, because I knew that my priceless herd of cows was in that barn. Within minutes I was as close to the inferno as possible, trying to look into flaming windows and door openings. No sound could be heard except the crackling of the timber, hay, and straw. I am thankful that I did not hear the frightful sounds of suffering animals. By daylight the flames had subsided, to reveal the horrifying picture of the remains of two rows of my most prized earthly possessions, securely fastened with their necks in well-anchored metal stanchions. The next day we dug a large hole with tractors and scoops and buried my cattle in a common grave, and my heart with them.

The shock and anguish put me in bed for several days. For weeks after that, I would walk aimlessly, alone at night, crying like a child and praying, "Why, oh why?" I had been in church all of my life. I had heard hundreds of sermons and had read much of the Scriptures and could quote some. But I just had not applied much of it to my own life, and I needed to learn some lessons if I was to be useful as a Christian in the years to come.

I had heard Matthew 6:19-21 both taught in Sunday School and preached from the pulpit, and I had read it from the Bible myself: "Lay not up for yourselves treasures upon earth, where moth and rust doth corrupt, and where thieves break through and steal:

"But lay up for yourselves treasures in heaven, where neither moth nor rust doth corrupt, and where thieves do not break through nor steal:

"For where your treasure is, there will your heart be also."

It was while I was walking and crying myself sick that it dawned on me that these verses were for me and I would have to accept them. Only then did I find peace and reconciliation.

During the next thirty-five years, I have owned two or three hundred dairy cows and some were more productive and valuable than the ones I lost. But one thing is certain — I never did treasure them. They always remained just some more dairy cattle. Now, years later, I look back upon this grim experience as one of the best things that ever happened to me.

CHAPTER FIVE
AN APPETITE FOR MISSIONS

I cannot recall when I did not hold missions and missionaries in high esteem, yet neither my wife nor I personally knew a missionary until late summer 1952.

For many years I taught a Sunday School class for high school and college age young people in the country church we attended. I included what I had read and learned about the subject of missions. I got the name and address of a young national preacher in India and corresponded with him to learn some of his needs. Then I urged our class to assume a project, and we bought him a bicycle. The church's missions program was set up for members to contribute through the denominational missionary fund. Funds received were then distributed by the church mission board to both home and foreign workers. Both my wife and I found this method of supporting missions very dull and impersonal, and we longed for a more challenging way to express our enthusiasm.

In the late fall of 1951, a friend invited us one Sunday evening to visit a church he frequently attended. The music was great, and the preacher presented the first really stirring message on missions we had ever heard. Our hearts burned within us, and whenever we were free, we attended Sunday evening services there.

The more we heard about the priority of foreign missions, the deeper our Christian life became. It even affected our lifestyle and pattern. The next spring, when I would finish planting or sowing a field of grain, I would drive my tractor to the gate to leave with my implements. But before leaving, I began a practice of kneeling by my tractor wheel and thanking the Lord for the sowing of the seed, asking Him for a plenteous harvest, and promising Him a generous portion of the increase brought by the early and late rains. I always kept my promise, and I never experienced a crop failure.

We lived in a weather belt where spring storms and hail were commonplace and often destructive. Many farmers carried hail insurance on their crops, which they kept in force until they were harvested. It was expensive insurance, but I also took out this coverage on my crops, just as others in the area. One spring, just before time to take out crop insurance, the thought hit me that if I belonged to the Lord, so also did my crops. I should be trusting Him for crop protection from hail and storm, just as I trusted Him for rains to make them grow. By this time we had come to know of a missionary who was headed for South America. So we trusted the Lord for protection from hail and put the amount of the insurance premium into missions toward the support of our new acquaintance. Our crops never suffered any hail damage, and the missions program received the benefit.

Over the Labor Day weekend in 1952, friends invited us to attend a church retreat at a nearby camp. These folks attended a missionary-minded church which was beginning to exercise a strong influence on our thinking. We accepted the invitation. On Sunday afternoon, the church held a commissioning service for a young couple going to serve as their missionaries in Chile, South America. After we listened to Bob and Barbara tell about the Chileans, their deep needs, and how they planned to serve, the couple knelt and the elders of the church, with the pastor, surrounded them. As these men laid hands on the heads of the departing missionaries, the pastor charged the couple to go under God's guidance, protection, and blessing.

Something came over me that afternoon that I cannot explain or understand. I was a strong man in my late forties and not easily moved, yet I began to weep. I continued to do so throughout the entire service, and nothing I did could stop that flow of tears. I was really embarrassed, but I kept on crying until after the last amen was said. Looking back on that experience, I believe it was the first step toward what was to happen to us seven years later, in mid-January, 1959, in Mexico. It seems impossible, but Bob and Barbara were the first missionaries we had ever seen. I suppose that tender spot that was in my heart toward foreign missions was touched, because the Lord had been leading up to this experience for some time, and for a purpose.

One does not easily tear up roots and transplant them to a new soil. On the other hand, if one is a Christian, he does not ignore the leading of the Lord in the matter of change. After much pondering and prayer, our family moved our church membership into this other church in July, 1952. We were soon involved in its activities and interests. In fifteen years I held a number of offices and served as a member of most of the boards and committees.

Soon, instead of knowing one missionary couple, we knew two — then five, ten, twenty. We heard dynamic missionary speakers: R. R. Brown, Franklin Logsdon, Darlene Rose, Lloyd Van Stone, Alan Redpath, Oswald J. Smith, Paul Van Gorder — all pounding home the theme that taking God's Word to those who have not yet heard is the Lord's priority. It soon became our priority, too. We began praying for and helping to support Christian workers all around the world, and we began honoring God with at least 20% of our income.

We marvelled, as our income increased to more than cover our missionary faith-promise pledges. We experienced our first thrills in adventurous giving. Missionary conferences in our church were times of happiness and revival. We could scarcely believe that we were the ones who were moving so rapidly along this new road. Truly, we were ever learning and coming gradually to the knowledge of the truth.

CHAPTER SIX
THE TOURIST ROUTE PLUS

By 1957 I had become the senior partner in the farming business. Our land lay directly in the path of progress and development because of the mushroom growth of Indianapolis. Two parcels of land had become too valuable to farm, so I set about developing them into subdivisions for homesites. The first was a small, sparsely-wooded tract, favorably located and easy to prepare. It became popular and sold out the first year at a considerable profit. The second area, a larger tract, demanded more detail, time, and overhead, along with the exercise of better management and more imagination. But I applied what I had learned the year before, solving one problem or detail at a time, and soon things fell into place. The second enterprise progressed on schedule to become another successful project, completed a few years later with rewarding satisfaction and profit.

Early in 1959, my wife and I decided that we needed a few weeks' rest from our activities and responsibilities. We made plans to drive to Mexico for two weeks, and intended when we returned to the U.S. border, to go to California for another couple of weeks. Little did we know the strange and new experiences the Lord had for us that would change our lives, attitudes and outlook. We were to enter a new world — but not California.

Within half an hour after we crossed the bridge over the Rio Grande into Matamoros, Mexico, I had learned three things. First, Mexican streets and roads are poorly marked. Second, I had forgotten all the Spanish I had learned in college. And third, I couldn't communicate with the pedestrians and bystanders — they didn't understand my brand of English. I turned around to get off that dead-end street and went back to try one that did not look so promising but did happen to lead into Highway 101 toward Victoria, then turned left onto Route 85 to Mexico City.

When we came to the sign marked "Tropic of Cancer," I thought we must be nearing the equator. I got out with my camera to take a picture of this important place, but all there was besides the sign were a mare donkey and two colts trying to share the shade of a lone cactus with three longhorn steers. I hardly knew what I expected to see, but anyway I was disappointed. I took a picture of the sign, however.

At six o'clock the evening of the next day I drove into the garage of the Del Prado Hotel in the heart of downtown Mexico City, bone-weary and one scared **hombre**. We would not have been able to do it, had it not been for a kind Mexican guide who was driving guests, sightseeing in the mountains up north. They were having lunch in the town of Jacala, and by good fortune, we found that his guests were staying at the Del Prado and were on their way to Mexico City also. We were welcome to follow them to the hotel if we wished. No one will ever know how much I wished. But alas, no one can know what it is like to follow a Mexican driver through the mountains, villages, plains, pedestrians, animals and carts, if he has not tried it. It is a great way to test your driving skills, nerves, blood pressure, and temper. It is truly an unforgettable experience to drive from Teotihuacan in the north suburbs to the Del Prado Hotel on Juarez in the center of the city, either following a guide or on your own, at 6 p.m. For eight days thereafter, walking was a pleasure. My wife recovered first, even though she had been sitting on the edge of the car seat for two days.

We observed that coming 700 miles from the border, we passed through a new world almost every 100 miles. In each world we noticed that the people dressed differently from the previous one. There were two things that appeared to be common to all, however. People walked both ways along the highway or waited in little groups by the roadside, all with somber faces — and everyone carried a load on his or her back. Farm people from the Midwest are not accustomed to seeing people carrying heavy loads on their backs, with faces revealing heavy burdens in their hearts. We pitied them and wondered where they were going or where they had been.

The next morning at 9 a.m. the telephone rang in our room. Enrique Mora announced that he was in the hotel lobby to meet us, as had been arranged, as soon as we wished to come down.

At our AAA office in Indianapolis, a reliable English-speaking guide had been recommended to us by someone who had engaged his services in Mexico City the previous year. Henry, his English name, lives on Rio Rhin Street. He was available, and we had our Indianapolis office engage him as our guide for eight days, beginning at 9 a.m. of this our first day in Mexico City.

It was agreed that Henry would chauffeur us around in our car each day, leaving the hotel about 9 a.m. and returning us there between 4 and 5 p.m. He would show us the tourist sights and attractions from the Pyramids on the north or Cuernavaca and Taxco on the south, and from Toluca in the west to Pueblo and Vera Cruz in the east — and everything in between. And we really saw it all, including Chapultepec Castle, University City, the floating gardens of Xochimilco, the Shrine of Guadalupe, famous murals, the Latin American Tower, and the Thieves' Market. We also witnessed some local entertainments, such as the Folklorico Ballet, a cockfight and a bullfight. Every evening we returned burdened with goodies of leather, silver, glass, onyx, and baskets galore to please family and friends.

Henry proved to be a good driver, an excellent guide, and a true friend. One evening he took us home to meet his wife Josefina, and Chico, his five year old son. A day or two later he decided to take Chico with us on a trip to Cholula. It was a great idea for thirty minutes, or until Chico took a turn at our car radio, running it full blast. But we also had some quiet times, since we visited more than a dozen cathedrals of every size, age, and description. Cholula has 365 cathedrals, one for each day of the year.

Henry was also a fine teacher. We even learned to pronounce Quetzalcoatl, the feathered serpent, and Popocatepetl, the gallant volcanic warrior lovingly guarding his sleeping lady, Ixtacihuatl. Thus, for $8.00 U.S. per day plus tips, we received a liberal arts education and many pleasant memories. It was with

30

real regret that we sincerely thanked Henry for his services and bade him goodbye. We were especially grateful for Henry, because on the morrow — on, no! not again! — and thereafter, I would have to drive that car through the city of six million people, with one-third of them on the streets every day.

During our stay at the Del Prado Hotel, we almost always had an early dinner in the Pom Pom restaurant, a pretty little place on the street floor of the Del Prado. Most Mexicans do not have dinner until quite late in the evening, and most dining rooms opened too late to suit our eating habits.

One evening, as we were having dinner at the Pom Pom, we noticed a Stateside couple and two little girls, as they came in and were seated. They ordered their food and then conversed until it was served. Before they ate, however, they bowed their heads while the husband returned thanks to God for the food. Our hearts rejoiced, because that was our family custom, whether we ate in public or in private. But these were the first people we had seen in Mexico who gave thanks at the table.

We finished our meal and passed their table as we were leaving the dining room. We stopped, introduced ourselves, and thanked them for their public Christian testimony. We told them it was our practice also to thank God for our blessings before we ate, and what a pleasure it was to find someone with whom we shared this custom, especially in a foreign land.

We agreed later that this meeting was not merely accidental. It seemed to us that the Lord arranged to bring this family into our lives at this exact time, place, and under these circumstances. Meeting Reverend and Mrs. Bob Collett and their two young daughters was a truly delightful experience. Bob was with Youth for Christ, International, of Wheaton, Illinois. He had been sent to Mexico for several months to set up plans for the 11th World Congress of the organization.

Bob fired questions at us so fast that we could hardly answer them. "What are you doing in Mexico? Where are you staying? How long are you going to be here? What have you seen? When can we spend some time with you?"

We explained that we were staying at the Del Prado, that our time in Mexico City was growing short, and that we would welcome a visit from them. Since Bob had a speaking engagement that evening and must leave for it as soon as they finished dinner, we suggested, "What about tomorrow evening — same time, same place?" They assented, "Just great! We'll see you then."

At 5 o'clock the next evening we met and enjoyed a meal together. It was a cheerful occasion, as we exchanged stories of our experiences and predicaments encountered in the past few days. Our dinner was well seasoned with jokes and laughter. We found that the Colletts had left a pastorate to assume duties with Youth for Christ for a time. They had experience also in radio broadcasting, as Mrs. Collett and the children had produced a Saturday morning program for several years. In turn, they learned about our farm background, our children, our church, and our home. After dinner we continued our conversation as we took a stroll on the Avenue Juarez, window-shopping and watching the people come and go.

As we talked, the subject came up of what we planned to do with the rest of our time in Mexico. We outlined for them our plans for the next few days. We would go to Acapulco where we would spend four nights at the Prado Americus Hotel. Then we would return to Mexico City, stay overnight, cross the border by Route 57, and then turn west to visit Los Angeles for a couple of weeks.

"Aren't there other things in Mexico you haven't seen?" they asked. "Since we've been here awhile, surely there is something we can show you. When you come back from Acapulco, let's try to work something more in before you leave."

"Okay if we extend your stay for a couple more days?" Bob Collett urged.

We explained the mail and contact stations we had established along the route to California, where our daughter could reach us any day by phone or letter, and that we had learned to travel and stay on a schedule because we felt more secure in doing so. The Colletts were understanding when they heard our reasons for continuing on our way, but still Bob persisted, "If you did have more time in Mexico, what would you like to do and see that you have not already enjoyed?" After a moment's consideration, I replied, "While we were in Indianapolis, we heard there were mission fields in Mexico. Often we've thought we'd like to visit a mission field some day. I suppose we would like to do that, if we had more time."

"I know just the place!" Bob exulted. "It's the scene of the greatest missionary story we've ever heard!"

Curious by this time, I asked him, "Have you ever been there?"

"Yes," he assured us, "a couple of times. The people are the Otomi and their spiritual leader is named Venancio. The story of his life is a miracle in itself. I sure wish you could go and see Otomi country. It would be the highlight of your trip to Mexico!"

Pondering the feasibility of rerouting ourselves to the border, I inquired "How does one get there?" His reply indicated that he had the same thought in mind. "It's between here and the border," he explained, "about two hours' drive north on the Pan American Highway." We wished we had known this on the way down because that was the way we came. But we must go on to Acapulco, we felt, because our reservations were paid for at the Prado Americus. "It's a pity we can't cram everything into two weeks, but we just can't," I told him regretfully.

"I understand how these things happen, and how time gets away," Bob agreed. "But we still have another hour or two to walk and talk. By the way, have you ever heard of the Wycliffe Bible Translators?"

We had to confess we'd never heard of them and asked if they were missionaries. Bob explained that Mexico did not allow missionaries in the country, but Wycliffe workers were students and scientists, specializing in linguistics. These linguists worked only among tribespeople who had no written languages, for the purpose of learning the languages, writing them down, and giving the people dictionaries, primers of appropriate literature, and teaching them to read and write. Ultimately the goal of these linguists was to translate for the people the entire New Testament in their own tongue. "That's good work, pleasing to God, by whatever name you call it," Bob concluded. "And it really works. It opens to them God's Word that sets them free." He added that there were Wycliffe Bible Translators working among the Otomi in nothern Mexico, and there were at that time more than a hundred believers living at a place called Colony Hill.

"This sounds like the kind of place that would interest us immensely, and we'd like to visit there sometime — but not on this trip," I decided reluctantly. But for an hour thereafter Bob told us exciting highlights of Otomi Christian experiences as Ethel Wallis, a Wycliffe author, had related them in her book, **Otomi Shepherdess**. Ethel Wallis had worked at Tetzu, a village ten miles north of the town of Ixmiquilpan, in the heart of Otomi country, for many years. She knew and loved these charming people, Bob said, and they in turn respected and loved her. She had especially been a great help to Venancio, the Otomi Christian leader. To sum up his account, he added, "And Ethel Wallis is here in Mexico City now; we saw her last week. We would like to introduce you to her — in fact, there are many missionaries here we would like to have you meet when you get back in town. Perhaps we can have another hour together; at least, we'll want to say goodbye before you leave on Tuesday." We were happy to agree to this, thanked them for such a delightful evening, and returned to our rooms to start packing to leave for Acapulco early the next morning. But we got little sleep that night; our minds were full of the story of the Otomi living on Colony Hill.

We enjoyed every minute of Acapulco. The view from our hotel was breathtaking, the food was out of this world, the gardens surpassed imagination in beauty, while the city and surroundings were unique and fascinating. Driving was easy, shopping was delightful, and people were friendly. Our visit proved to be enjoyable in every way, except for all the nearly sleepless nights. The story of those Otomi continually revolved in our minds, and we reviewed it over and over — the experiences of Venancio and his Colony of believers. By Sunday noon, we couldn't stand it any longer. By a telephone call we told our daughter in Indianapolis of this new obsession. We then cancelled our trip to California and made up our minds to stay at least two more weeks in Mexico. We would meet members of Wycliffe Bible Translators and explore Otomi country to determine its powerful attraction. With that decision arrived at, that night we slept soundly.

CHAPTER SEVEN
UNEXPECTED ACQUAINTANCES

We returned to Mexico City exactly on schedule. On Monday afternoon we checked in at our hotel and I called the Colletts immediately, as we had promised. When he answered, I said, "Guess what?" Bob answered, "That's easy — you're going to stay over to meet the Wycliffe members and the Otomi. By the way, since you have nothing planned, how would you like to go to prayer meeting Wednesday night at the Wycliffe headquarters here in the city?"

"Fine — we'd like to go," I said. "But you owe us a bunch of money for the loss of four nights sleep."

The Colletts took us to the Wycliffe headquarters the following afternoon to meet some of the members. Our arrival was timed perfectly. Just as we entered, this charming young lady came down the stairway with a book in her hand. It was Ethel Wallis, and as soon as we were introduced, she held out the book and offered it to us. "This is for you," she told us. "I understand you would like to visit the Otomi of the Mezquital. Here is a copy of **Otomi Shepherdess,** and it will acquaint you with what to expect when you go." This was the first author we had ever met, and she had already autographed the book. Our first impression of the Wycliffe Bible Translators was auspicious, and soon we were to meet Dr. Benjamin Elson, Mexico Branch Director for Wycliffe, and his gracious wife Adelle. We were also introduced to Katie Voigtlander, Peggy Wendell, Olga Warner, Bill and Marj Nyman, Howard and Bea Klassen, Bill and Jay Upson, Dorothy White, Helen Ashdown, Alan and Iris Wares, Cloyd and Ruth Stewart, and a score or more lovely and personable missionaries. Never had we expected to meet so many all in one place. This one afternoon had made the cancellation of our previous plans worthwhile.

Dr. Elson took us to his office to show us wall maps marked with thumb tacks placed where 285 Wycliffe translators were working in Mexico at that time. He showed us samples of Scripture portions that had already been translated into languages of various tribes, as well as fascinating artifacts, including some from the Otomi.

After a time, the conversation turned to our desire to visit the Otomi at Ixmiquilpan, and immediately Bill and Marj Nyman invited us together with Bob Collett to accompany them on a trip they planned to take two days later to the Mezquital Valley. This arrangement exactly suited us all. We returned to our hotel, had dinner, read our new book, and then stayed awake half the night recalling the delightful afternoon we had spent, and the miracles narrated in the book Ethel Wallis had given us.

The following evening we returned to the Wycliffe headquarters (named by Wycliffe members "The Kettle," an abbreviation of its former name, "Palace of Quetzlcoatl"), for the prayer meeting. We recognized new friends made the previous day, but also saw many unfamiliar faces in the room which was full to overflowing. Apparently we were the only guests. After a song or two and an invocation, one of the members gave a report of his recent experiences in his village allocation and mentioned prayer needs relative to his work and people. When two or three other translators had given reports and named specific prayer requests, the moderator then asked someone to pray for the needs mentioned. An hour or more was spent covering such reports and detailing needs for prayer, such as problems in the villages, persecuted believers, sickness, etc., as well as matters for rejoicing and praise. We could not but feel the dedication of this group of Christians, every one of whom appeared to have a similar zeal for his task. We perceived that we were getting a taste of what prayer meetings were intended to achieve.

On the Pan American Highway, this is Dios Padre, a warm pool fed by a stream overflowing a hot mineral spring. The Otomí women wash their clothes and hang them on a bush to dry. They bathe and scrub the kids also. When a car slows down or stops at the roadside, the Otomí dive underwater like ducks.

CHAPTER EIGHT
A DREAM COME TRUE

The next morning at 10 o'clock as prearranged, Bill and Marj Nyman with Bob Collett picked us up in their car, and we drove north on No. 85 for the hundred-mile drive to Kilometer 159. This was the same road on which we had traveled down into Mexico two weeks before, but this time we noted every detail, as Bill Nyman called our attention to dozens of new and interesting things. He pointed out the maguey cactus and told us of its nutritional virtues and alcoholic vices — in fact, its some one hundred uses by the Otomi people. He showed us granaries built up in the trees to preserve their contents from the goats, the silver mines of Pachuca, people spinning wool thread as they walked to market or herded goats in the fields. We noted people washing clothes or bathing in the warm spring water at the roadside of Dios Padre, the black water irrigation canals, and many other interesting things, as they appeared. None of these had we had time to investigate, as we followed the Mexican guide at full speed into the city. The drive to Ixmiquilpan we found very exciting the first time we explored it, and it remains so to us still. Today, however, the road has been much improved, until it drops into the Mezquital Valley.

It was noon when we arrived at the town. Directly on the highway stood a filling station, with a quaint and unique seven-room motel on the property and a surprisingly good restaurant, the whole establishment called simply "Dobbs." The story was that a number of years ago a young man from the States came through the area, hunting a promising location to go into business. In due time he met and fell in love with a Mexican senorita and married her. Both were capable, energetic and possessed of business sense. Mr. and Mrs. Dobbs saw that Ixmiquilpan could become the main stop between Tamazunchale, just north of the Sierra Madre range of mountains, and Mexico City. They built the filling station, motel, and restaurant, and their establishment became well-known and prosperous. Called just plain "Dobbs," it was the place where Bill and Marj chose to stop for lunch. Since the first visit, my wife and I have stopped there dozens of times. Mr. Dobbs had died before our first visit, but after a time we came to know Mrs. Dobbs, and soon we were close friends. She was a good woman and always very pleasant to us.

After lunch we set off again to accomplish our purpose for coming. Within two blocks of Dobbs, we turned into the narrowest, roughest, steepest, and dirtiest street we had ever seen in our lives. Since rain fell only rarely, the roads were covered

37

A mezquite tree with a granary built in the upper limbs to keep goats from raiding, eating, and spoiling the grain.

with two inches of reddish-grey dust. We were now on our way up Colony Hill to visit Venancio and the believers who lived there, almost in the shadow of a Government Army Post.

In ten minutes we reached Venancio's house, only to find that there was not a man on Colony Hill just then. They were all working that day on a road in the vicinity of Villa Gran, a method by which they discharged their tax obligation. My wife and I felt like two kids who had stayed up all night waiting for Santa Claus, only to discover that it lacked a day of being Christmas. We felt better, however, when we learned that they would return by 4 o'clock. Meanwhile, we drove ten or twelve miles up the road to visit the villages of Tasquillo and Tetzu. Tasquillo proved to be a beautiful town, sitting in a grove of the largest pecan trees we had ever seen. We drove past the house where Bill and Marj had lived at one time, and beyond it we passed through the most gorgeous cactus forest in Mexico, on the way to see a handmade swinging bridge across the Tula River — for the use of the people only, but a few goats made use of it too, we were told. In the town of Tasquillo we visited a charming Wycliffe couple and their children, Harwood and Pat Hess. In a few minutes' time, we became warm friends.

Up the road a couple of miles from Tasquillo is Tetzu, a typical Otomi village, well-hidden in the cactus. The simple and crude homes are made of reeds, stalks, and organ cactus walls, with maguey cactus leaves for roots. If one stands and looks around, he cannot see more than two or three huts because they are so well concealed among the dense growth of tall cactus. Here we visited Ethel Wallis's home, built of stone and tile when she first came to the Mezquital. Nancy Lanier, a translator from California, was occupying the house at the time. She invited us in for a rest, and then took us to see her Otomi neighbor who was carding black wool in preparation for spinning thread and weaving clothing for her family. We concluded that Mexico was a fascinating place in which to live — so many new and strange things to see, impossible to take all of them in during one visit.

It seemed that these Otomi were now living probably as they had a hundred years ago, except that now they could walk to Tasquillo and exchange three eggs for a pint bottle of kerosene — provided they have the bottle and the three eggs.

Then we hurriedly drove back to Ixmiquilpan and up to Colony Hill to see if the men had arrived yet. We arrived in time to meet Don and Isabel Sinclair, a Wycliffe couple who also make their home on the Hill because by living there, they can be available to help the church, the pastor, and the people. Isabel plays a small portable organ for all occasions at the church or anywhere

39

This is the first colony church that was built by the believers from stone they dug and shaped in the desert. It seated 150 persons. The original land purchased, "Chapultepec" was presented and dedicated here.

Women's choir directed by Isabel Sinclair, standing in the back row. Isabel dresses like the Otomi women.

else in the community where it may be required. Don and Isabel not only write materials for the Sunday Schools, but they teach adult reading classes, taxi jeep station-wagon loads of people to nearby congregations and back at almost any hour of the day or night. Never a problem arises but that Don will give it a listening ear and a helping hand.

The Sinclairs walked with us to visit the church. The brethren had gone into the desert, dug stone, and brought it up the hill to build this pretty little church which seats some 150 people on wooden backless benches. The men sit on the right and the women on the left of the center aisle. The stones had been neatly laid with the joints smooth, and painted on the outside a pale turquoise. The single door, in the center front, was gently arched, and above the arch in large letters were the words, "Iglesia Cristiana Independiente." As we stepped inside the door, our conversation automatically became hushed whispers. No one had suggested this, but we had the feeling that loud voices were out of place, even though no service was being held. We had never before been in a church where we felt such an atmosphere of worship as we did here.

As we walked through the narrow streets toward Venancio's house, we noted that the house of every believer was built of the same desert stone as the church, except that in the houses, the stone remained in its natural gray color. Some children peeped out of doorways, while bolder ones followed us — but at a safe distance. Beautiful children, they were — the kind you'd like to pick up and squeeze. An outstanding trait of these children of Otomi believers is that they do not beg. They have been carefully trained that it is wrong to beg and unbecoming to believers' families, since they have a loving Heavenly Father who provides what they need. Colony Hill children are some of the best-mannered we have found anywhere.

When we reached Venancio's house again, his wife Celedonia came out to greet the Sinclairs and to meet the North American visitors. We had timed our arrival well, because a little after 4 o'clock we heard a vehicle bumping and rattling up the hill, enveloped in a cloud of dust. The truck stopped right in front

Tele and Sabina and little daughter . . . a most lovely successful Otomi family. This was taken at Gamio Linguistic Center at Ixmiquilpan when perhaps there were only two buildings erected. Tele was the caretaker and watchman. Since then he has prepared himself and worked into a responsible position in the area Mexican-Otomi school system.

of us and discharged twenty-five or thirty men who had been holding onto the truck rack. Each wore a straw hat and a smiling face, covered with dust. They didn't just bail out like a bunch of schoolboys, but climbed down quietly and politely greeted the Nymans, Bob Collett, and the Sinclairs whom they knew, and then were introduced to the **gringos** who were complete strangers. Each followed Venancio's example and with hat in hand, each shook hands with both friends and newcomers. They didn't immediately excuse themselves to go home, wash, and change their clothes. By this time, the wives and children had gathered to join the crowd at the side of the truck. There appeared to be about a hundred people in all.

Bill Nyman spoke to Venancio in Spanish, and he in turn interpreted to the group in Otomi. Then Bill gave it back to us in English. During this conversation, Bill and Marj told the Otomi group that it was always a pleasure to visit the Colony on the Hill, but especially so at this time when the purpose for coming was to bring the Dawsons who had so wished to visit the Otomi that they had cancelled a scheduled trip to California to allow time for the trip. The people expressed pleasure and hoped that we had found the visit worthwhile enough for the change of plans. They counted our visit an honor, and were only sorry that all the men had to be gone when we came.

As the conversation continued for another half-hour, we realized that we were looking into an entirely different kind of faces than the ones we met along the road as we drove down into Mexico, or even along the streets of Ixmiquilpan. These people responded to our smiles and compliments on their church, their stone houses, and their beautiful children. They might be poor, but they were not impoverished. They were relaxed and content, while their beautiful features reflected a charming poise. These were the kind of people we had hoped to see as a result of the work on the mission field. The Colony men worked for wealthy Mexicans, for a customary wage of five or six **pesos** per day, yet they were able to manage a living for their families because they no longer drank, fought, gambled, lied, or stole. They had a strong faith and lived by it.

It was time for us to leave and drive back to Mexico City, if we were to arrive in time for dinner. Bill Nyman explained to Venancio and asked if the people would consent to sing for us. He also asked Venancio to pray for our safe return. The group sang **a capella** a sweet, beautiful song. The pastor closed his eyes and lifted his face before I could bow my head. I realized then why God wanted us to come here instead of going to California. I heard his soft, quiet voice, but I do not know what he prayed

43

because it was in Otomi. But we felt that surely God knew, and it moved us greatly in our hearts.

Quickly we said goodbye to the Sinclairs, to the Otomi, their families, and Pastor Venancio, while they in turn thanked us for our visit and warmly invited us to come again. As we drove back to Mexico City, voices were subdued and there was less small talk and idle chatter. Our hearts burned within us again — at last we had seen what was being accomplished on the mission field. We were most grateful to our friends for exposing us to this new experience. It recalled to us the Sunday afternoon in 1952 when we saw our first missionaries commissioned. Both experiences created the same feeling of awe in our hearts.

CHAPTER NINE
SUPPOSE THEY HAD A CHANCE

When we returned from Acapulco, we decided to change hotels. Henry had explained that there was a place called "Shirley Courts" on Sullivan which was easily accessible by car. Jim Shirley, the owner and operator, had succeeded his father who had located there several years ago. He was a Texan and took pains to see that food and water were protected from contamination. Cars were parked in an enclosed garage and well guarded. People came from every state in the Union and returned year after year. Since it was more convenient for us than the hotel downtown, it became our home to which we returned on our many trips in future years. From there, we began to use taxis to get around the city, to go downtown, to the markets, to church, and to Wycliffe headquarters.

We told the Wycliffe folks how much we had been impressed by the Otomi, and that we would like to pay them another visit as soon as possible. This time, however, we would like to drive our own car and go by ourselves because we wanted to take a closer, more leisurely look. No one at the headquarters could answer our question, "What would happen if the Otomi believers had one good chance in life?" Probably none of them could actually realize what it was like to look at these people through the eyes of a farmer.

Soon after that, we packed an overnight bag and drove out to Ixmiquilpan, strictly on our own. In about two hours we arrived at Dobbs' where we took a room in their quaint motel and

Don and Isabel Sinclair in their patio enclosure standing beside their yellow Jeep station wagon called "Heavenly Sunshine." This is about half way up Colony Hill.

parked our car securely in an enclosure. We ate our lunch there, and then unannounced we walked up the steep hill to ring the bell on the Sinclairs' wall gate. They were at home and cordially invited us in. By way of explanation, we told them that our previous visit had been much too brief. There were aspects of Otomi life we wanted to learn about, and further information that we needed on some points. Would they serve as our guides and interpreters, as we took another look? They gladly consented to drop what they were doing and help us as long as we wished.

But now, for the first time in our experience, we were up against the barrier which an unknown language raises between the peoples of the world. So Don and Isabel began that day a task that would take two or three years, and which would enlist the help of Nancy Lanier, Teke (Harwood) and Pat Hess, Ethel Wallis, and Pat Cowan in interpreting our English to the Otomis and their Otomi to us. I am sure that we tried the patience of our interpreters many times, but they were so gracious as to act as if it was nothing.

Off we went again for a more detailed visit to Colony Hill. We started at Venancio's house, where we found that the largest loom on the Hill had been installed on Venancio's porch so that anyone who wanted to learn to weave could be taught. Another item of interest which Celedonia proudly displayed was the baby hammock. By means of an attached cord, it could be swung by someone sitting at a distance. As we sat a few minutes, looking

45

Nancy Lanier (left) and Pat Cowan (right) rejoicing over a surprise bag of groceries stacked on their front porch table at Tetzu.

Dr. Harwood (Teke) and Pat Hess relaxing at Shirley Courts Motel in Mexico City.

across the patio through pots of blooming flowers on the bannisters, discussing the church and its part in their lives, we found that there was a church service every night of the week. In the absence of newspapers, radios, televisions, even telephones — the life of the community centered around the church. We heard about neighboring congregations pastored by laymen, trained by Venancio. When I asked, "How many young Timothys do you have?" he answered, "Eight."

We next walked down to Tito's house to meet Lazara, his wife. She was weaving on a primitive loom of medium size which hung from a wall of the house, under the roof of an open porch. The rebozo she was weaving was of unusual design and beauty. Baby turkeys ran back and forth under the loom as she worked, and a baby pig slept peacefully on the floor. Tito, the assistant pastor, is Venancio's cousin. He and his wife are a smiling couple.

Near the top of the Hill lives Teofilo and his family. Teofilo had endured severe and vicious persecution a few years before, simply because he and his son left the traditions and teaching of their forefathers to become believers and followers of this new faith. Hot-headed radicals caught and bound both Teofilo and his 19 year old son. They were given an instant ultimatum to renounce their new belief, and both refused. Teofilo saw his son brutally killed before his eyes, while he was bound and could do nothing to defend the boy. This is such a story as one reads about in Bible times, but doesn't expect to have happen today. Hearing about this actual martyrdom gave us a strange feeling, and we searched our own hearts as to whether or not we would be willing to pay such a price for our faith. We have since learned of two further acts of violence which have taken the lives of Otomi believers, one at White Stone, the other at Defai. We give thanks that we have never had to face such tests.

CHAPTER TEN
A GARDEN OF EDEN

A hundred yards beyond Teofilo's house is the highest point of Colony Hill. Standing at this outlook on the dry, barren path, we could see at least five miles to the west. In the distance we could see a row of sabino (cypress) trees outlining the course of the

Tula River, as it gently curved in our direction and then half a mile north of us passed under the Pan American Highway at the northern edge of Ixmiquilpan. As the river wended its way so near to us, we could see clearly the gigantic old trees along its banks. They appeared to be at least 400 years old — real patriarchs. This is the river that winds in and out of the Mezquital Valley, yet benefits only a small area of it. It rushes down from higher ground, a swiftly-flowing stream. A few miles out of Ixmiquilpan, on a plateau, irrigation canals have been cut, channelling life-giving water in every direction — even to parts of Ixmiquilpan — but none of it reaches Colony Hill. At the foot of the Hill everything is lush and green. Ten feet above the highest canal, everything is dry and barren. Cactus is the only green thing existing there. From where we stand, looking as far as one can see in every direction, fields of all sizes make a giant patchwork done in shades of green, with every kind of growing crop imaginable. These highly desirable pieces of land, very productive and quite expensive, belong to wealthy Mexicans. The altitude is right, the sun is hot because of the latitude, and the only missing element is water — to make it a Garden of Eden. That was exactly what we were seeing.

Gazing out over this paradise through the eyes of a farmer, one who loves the soil and has lived by it, I said to my wife, "Instead of asking, 'What would happen if these lovely people had one good chance?' — the question should be, 'What would happen if these people had some land of their own?'." That afternoon I determined to get an answer to that question, if it took longer than our allotted two weeks.

We walked back to the Sinclairs' house where they graciously invited us to stay for supper. Since they urged us, we gladly accepted. After we had eaten, without any warning I dropped my bombshell.

"What would happen if the believers had some land of their own?" I asked Don and Isabel. After giving it some thought, they admitted they didn't know. "That question has never come up before," they finally replied. "Give it some thought and prayer," I suggested. "Could it help them, or would it be hurtful to them? I have a real purpose in asking."

The Sinclairs delivered us to the foot of the Hill in their jeep station wagon. At the restaurant we got a bottle of pure drinking water and went to our room. Our bed covers consisted of a clean white sheet and two wool blankets, each a quarter-inch thick and weighing ten pounds. We finally fell off to sleep despite the noises of burros, geese, yelping dogs, roosters, and church bells. Probably the sounds of a boiler factory could not have kept us awake.

Pastor Venancio and Celedonia, his wife, surveying the irrigation land, Chapultepec from the top of Colony Hill. This picture was taken when we were investigating the prospects and exploring the possibilities of buying it.

These cypress (sabino) trees on the banks of the Tula River were old trees even before the United States was born.

Next morning, after an excellent breakfast, we checked out of the motel where we had enjoyed a remarkably comfortable night's rest. Teke and Pat Hess showed some surprise at seeing us so soon, but we had felt that by all means we should drive up to Tasquillo while we were so near. Without hesitation, we admitted we had come to love the Otomi people, and there was a question revolving in our minds: "What would happen if the believers on Colony Hill owned some land of their own?" We told them that we had asked the Sinclairs, "Would owning land at this time help them or possibly do them some harm?" The Sinclairs hadn't been able to give us an answer, however. Perhaps they were not ready to say as yet. Teke and Pat said that when they came into Mexico City in a day or two, they would visit us at Shirley Courts, and then we would discuss this matter in detail, after all of us had had more time to consider all its implications.

Since Tetzu was only some two miles up the road, we drove there to talk with Nancy Lanier about the severe water shortage at her house. She faced the problem of carrying buckets of water at least half a mile from the cement storage tank which the government had built at the edge of the village.

Trucks similar to those used by stateside oil companies to deliver gasoline to farm tractors periodically brought water from the river to store in these government-built cement tanks. From there the villagers carried it to their homes. It seemed inconsistent to us that a busy Bible translator must carry household water each day. Her task is to translate God's Word and not "serve tables" (Acts 6:2).

Nancy went back to Dobbs' with us to have lunch, and in answer to our questions, took the opportunity to tell us more about the Otomi. It appeared that they were naturally musical. Nancy had just translated and published a hymnbook, which delighted the people because they love to sing. When we had to leave for Mexico City later in the afternoon, Nancy who had her own car went on her way. We found this trip to the Mezquital more exciting than our first visit, in that we had more time to observe in detail certain aspects of the situation and thus gained some new insights.

Since Ethel Wallis also has a vital interest in these people of the Mezquital for whom she is translating Scripture, the next morning we took a taxi to Wycliffe headquarters to have a talk with Ben Elson and Ethel who was there on a temporary assignment. She admitted us at the gate and of course was eager to know every detail of our two trips north and what our thoughts were now about the Otomi. It took us sometime before her curiosity was satisfied and we had answered all that she wanted to know. She was delighted and just beamed as we reported our happiness in our experiences. Then we asked her the new question which had developed out of the first one: "What would happen if the Otomi believers had some irrigation land of their own?" We discussed their capabilities, their relationships with the townspeople, their testimony, their leadership, and their ability to work together. Finally she commented, "It all seems like a dream — but a good dream. Why not ask Ben Elson what he thinks?" "We hoped to talk to both of you, and we saw you first," we said. "How do we go about seeing him? Will you lead the way?"

Happily, Dr. Elson was quite accessible and easy to talk to. He grinned at us as he asked how we got along with the Otomi on our own. We gave him a summary of the things we saw, heard and felt. We explained that the Lord had given us a warm spot in our hearts for them already, and we were somewhat disturbed over the seemingly helpless plight of the Colony believers. They were apparently caught in circumstances beyond their control, yet even in this situation, they possessed a rare poise that we greatly admired. Then I went on, "We have changed our tune a bit since we returned from our first trip. Now we keep asking ourselves, 'What would happen if these capable Otomi had some irrigation land of their own?' Would it spoil their testimony? Would it intensify the opposition of their critics? Would it give them a new respect for themselves? Would they be able to operate land successfully? Would it weaken or strengthen their church? Who knows? What do you think?"

He immediately replied, "The two church leaders are thoughtful and wise. I think you ought to ask them. I doubt if any outsider could answer your questions. Since Venancio and Tito are both bilingual, why don't we have them come here to the city? You can meet them in my office, and I'll be glad to translate English to Spanish and Spanish to English. You can speak to them about these things and at least have an interesting meeting."

We seized the opportunity at once and agreed, "The sooner, the better." Instantly Dr. Elson put in a long distance call to Isabel Sinclair, via Dobbs' service station at Ixmiquilpan. We waited a bit impatiently while a messenger was sent up Colony Hill to call Mrs. Sinclair to the phone. Within half an hour, however, she called Dr. Elson back, and we heard him say, "The Dawsons would like to talk to Venancio and Tito in my office tomorrow morning. Ten o'clock would be a good time for them. Will that give the Otomi brethren ample time to get here by bus? Then will you please relay the message and urge them to come? And thanks for your trouble."

Dr. Benjamin and Adelle Elson are pictured in this photograph enjoying a leisurely afternoon rest in our courtyard patio at Shirley Courts Motel, home away from home.

Miss Ethel Wallis — Translator, author, speaker, editor and lovely prayer partner.

CHAPTER ELEVEN

THEY GET THEIR CHANCE

We arrived at Ben Elson's office promptly at 10 o'clock the next morning, to find that Venancio and Tito were already there. After exchanging greetings and a few minutes chatting, our conversation turned to the purpose for summoning them there. Their faces betrayed no emotion, as we expressed our feelings, our interest and concern. After all, we were strangers, and many strangers had come to visit them in the past.

When the time seemed appropriate, I said, "We are farm people. We make our living and have educated our daughters by the use and fruits of the land. We have observed you and your people closely, and we believe you also would benefit from the use of your own land. We are believers and evangelicals like you, and we have discerned that God's hand is upon you. In the time we have known you, we have come to respect you greatly. Now there is a question to which we would like to have an answer. What would happen if you had some irrigation land of your own? We have called you here this morning to discuss this matter with you."

It took Dr. Elson several minutes to relate our words in Spanish. We have heard that a good interpreter not only communicates the words of the mouth but also expresses the thoughts and intents of the heart. Ben Elson undoubtly was a good interpreter. The Otomi men showed surprise but not elation. They did show serious interest, and I believe that at this time they recognized that our concern in their affairs was sincere. They appeared to relax and expressed their gratitude and appreciation.

Now the time seemed opportune to ask my questions, so I said to Ben, "Will you ask them these questions one at a time, and wait for answers from both of them? If suddenly you became owners of some land, would it spoil your testimony?" Both answered, "No, we do not think so. Our people are by nature of a mild disposition. We are founded and established in a strong faith. We do not easily become discouraged, nor do we think that we would become vain or proud if we were to be exalted. However, we have never yet been exalted, physically or materially."

"The next question is," I continued, "if you were suddenly to become landowners, would it intensify the ill feelings of your critics, the ones who hold grudges because you have embraced a new faith?" "We do not know for sure," they replied, "but it might work just the opposite way. We think that perhaps the majority of the townspeople, including critics, would have more respect for us if we became successful in something."

"Now my next question is," I went on, "if you had some irrigation land of your own, do your men know enough about farming to do a good job and keep it neat?" They responded, "All of us have worked in the fields at one time or another. Right now, about half of the brethren work in the fields for Mexican landowners, for five or six **pesos** a day (40¢-48¢ U.S.). To prepare, plant and tend the fields would be no new thing. We have been taught to be neat, and it seems we should have no difficulties."

Well satisfied with these careful answers, I turned to Dr. Elson. "Ben, will you ask them this last question: If you owned land, what would it do to your church — strengthen, weaken, or leave it the same?" They replied, "It couldn't help but strengthen it! Our church is filled now, and some day we will have to build a larger one. There are now new believers coming to us all the time. Most have lost their jobs because of their new faith, and some have taken refuge here because they had to flee persecution. Therefore there are more mouths to feed, plus the aged who can no longer work, and some who are ill. We have not known how we would manage in the future, but the people must be fed."

We continued to discuss details regarding all these questions for more than an hour. I asked Ben to say to the brethren, "It is a strange thing that the Lord led us so clearly to come to the Mezquital and see the need of the believers. He has shown us what irrigation has done for the land and has arranged for us to talk to you — the pastor and assistant pastor — about possibilities. Thank you for coming. I would like to ask you to go back home and call together at least six of your best leaders to meet with you and with us at the Sinclairs' house two days from today at 10:00 in the morning. I have a feeling that the Lord is going to give to my wife and me a missionary project of our own — not our church nor any mission board, but an agricultural missionary project between us and the Otomi believers. All of this, however, must be with full approval of Wycliffe Bible Translators, because they work among you. Okay?" Then I asked Ben to pray for us and these two leaders, as we attempted to pursue this matter to a conclusion. We ate lunch together in Wycliffe's dining room and then went our separate ways.

The next afternoon we drove to Dobbs' and registered into our motel room, thick blankets and all. We called Teke and Pat Hess and asked them to dinner with us so we could update them on our venture so far. Later, in our room, we all prayed together regarding the next morning's meeting at Sinclairs' house. Then feeling at peace about the outcome of the matter, we enjoyed a good night's rest.

The next morning by 10 o'clock we were at the Sinclairs'. When the Otomi men arrived and we all settled down to preliminaries and then the business of the meeting, our group almost filled the library-living room. We arranged that the Sinclairs would speak to the believers in Otomi and to us in English. This conference went on for three hours and more of tedious details. It took several minutes of palaver in Otomi to get back a short answer of "yes" or "no" in English. I finally asked that we speak in short sentences and answer in short sentences, confining ourselves to the subject exclusively, in order to conclude our business in the allotted time. So I ignored my own rule and led off with a long sentence. "All of us have expressed ourselves regarding this matter, and no one has brought up any reason why we should drop the subject. If my wife and I should decide to buy some irrigation land for your use, is there any for sale that you know of?" After a brief conference in Otomi, they replied, "Yes — an ex-president of the town has a piece of land that lies between the road to El Maye and the Tula River bank. He has two children in the university at Mexico City. School is about to start, and because he is short of money, he must sell something or take them out of school. For this reason, he is just now offering to sell the land which is called 'Chapultepec.' It contains five hectares (approximately ten acres)."

"Is it good land?" I wanted to know. "How much does he ask for it? Will he sell it to evangelicals?"

Venancio replied to the first question, with "Yes, it is very good land. I know about it because I have worked on it as a hired laborer many times." The other question no one could answer, so we sent a messenger on foot to get information from the owner himself. He was back in half an hour with a report. "Yes, it is for sale, and he must have 65,000 **pesos** ($5,200.00 U.S.). He will sell it to evangelicals if they have the money." Regarding the Colony believers, the owner of the property had commented: "I have watched you very closely for several years. You cause no one any trouble, you do not drink or fight, lie or steal, beg or annoy others — and I would be glad to sell it to you. Incidentally, this piece of ground was the first property we ever owned, and we are sorry to part with it."

Now we were getting down to serious business. The intent of our hearts was sincere, to the best of our knowledge, and now we must prove it. I now suggested, "Let's send our representative back to the gentleman and ask him how he wishes to have the money paid, if we decide to buy the land, and also how soon we may have possession of it." The Otomi men thought this a good idea, and off went the messenger again. He was gone a bit longer this time, it seemed to us, as we waited somewhat anxiously.

Finally he returned, bearing this message: "The land has wheat growing on it, and also a field of chili peppers. The owner wishes to harvest the crops when they are ready. He wishes to sell the land on a contract which provides these terms." (We recalled that this was also ordinary procedure in Indiana.) The messenger continued to relate the terms of the sale. "The purchasers should pay to him 20,000 pesos upon signing the contract. As soon as the wheat harvest is finished, probably in late spring (the chili peppers should be harvested before then), the other 45,000 pesos would be due. Then upon payment, the buyers would receive a deed and bona fide title and would have possession of the land at once."

I could see no flaw in this kind of deal and neither did the eight Otomi men. Being North Americans instead of Mexicans, I knew that my wife and I could not own property in Mexico, and we had no desire to, anyway, so I brought this up. "If we are led of the Lord into this business venture together, are you willing to form an association of eight men, appointing one to be trustee for the rest, to sign the contract, receive the title and deed, pay the annual irrigation water rights (100 pesos, or $8.00 U.S.), and pay the real estate tax for the association?" After discussing this at length, the Otomi men thought the association was a good idea, and they were willing. Then I concluded the matter with this final suggestion. "I will request that the pastor and the assistant pastor both be in the association," I said. "And the trustee can be whoever you choose. Let us send our representative to the landowner saying that we are interested, we believe his proposed arrangement is fair, and will he please give us until day after tomorrow at noon to make up our minds, sign the contract, and make the down payment."

By this time everyone in the room was exhausted and mopping their faces in the heat, especially the interpreters. We had prayer together, both in English and Otomi, and sent our delegate back to the landowner, while the rest of us walked down the road toward El Maye to see the piece of land called "Chapultepec."

Standing in the field of La Vina showing Colony Hill in the background with an Army post on top in the distance.

Author standing in the middle of a group of the land association members in a field that has been harvested.

Standing in a growing planted field in La Vina taken toward the road to El Maye.

Standing on the very edge of and taken across the first field "Chapultepec" with a mammoth pecan tree in the center.

An Otomi woman washes her clothes on a rock near the bank of the Tula River that borders our La Vina and Chapultepec fields. The river is a God-sent blessing to a dry and arid area. Our irrigation water comes from a higher elevation.

It was more beautiful than we had imagined, and the wheat and chili peppers looked promising, especially the wheat which occupied the larger field. Between the road and the field a fence had been built of thousands of stones, neatly stacked to form a wall four feet high and three feet wide. Some thirty feet from this wall, in the field of chili peppers, a stake had been driven into the ground. It looked about as large as a man's wrist and stood about six feet tall. Perched atop this stake sat the bleached skull of a goat, the nostril openings and eye sockets outlined with red paint. Having never come across anything like this before, I asked the Otomí men, "What's this?" They explained that the tenant had placed it there to ward off the effects of the evil eye of an insincere person passing by. He believed that the wrong person could cast an evil spell on his field and spoil his crop. "Little did this poor, ignorant farmer know that neither evil eyes, spells, nor spirits could damage chili peppers," I thought. "They are more potent than garlic." I could speak from personal experience.

I commented to the Otomí brethren, "Do you also believe in such things as this?" In reply they laughed and shook their heads. "Of course not. We have faith that the Lord will look after us. He would take care of our crops too, if we had any," they said.

We arranged to meet again at the Sinclairs' two days later, again at 10:00 a.m. Then we bade them goodbye and hurried to our car in order to reach Mexico City before dark. All the way back we mused on the happenings of the day and wondered how they would terminate.

The next morning we met with Ben Elson by appointment. We explained every detail of what had taken place and what was proposed. We asked if he could foresee any consequences or developments which might cause us regret or which might affect Wycliffe adversely. He answered that he felt the Lord had His hand on the entire plan and that he fully approved of our venture. I thanked him and told him, "Now we feel sure of ourselves. May we go to the finance office and get a check cashed for $1600.00 (20,000 pesos)?" "Sure — go ahead," he replied.

Bill Upson, the treasurer of Wycliffe's Mexico Branch, called Indianapolis to ask if we were worth $1600.00, and then counted out 20,000 pesos to me. When we left headquarters that afternoon, the roll of bills bulging my hip pocket resembled that of a Texas oilman.

The next morning we rose early, had breakfast, and by 8 o'clock were on our way to Ixmiquilpan. That day — February 25, 1959 — was to exert more influence over our future than any previous day of our lives. The experiences of that day gave us a new outlook — almost like getting a new member in the family.

When we arrived at the Sinclairs' house, the Otomi brethren were just getting there. For this meeting we had invited Teke Hess and Nancy Lanier to act as interpreters. Don and Isabel Sinclair sat next to us as alert observers of all. We opened the meeting with prayers in both English and Otomi from among those gathered in the crowded room. I reviewed the events of two days before, and asked the Otomi brethren for news of any new developments, or from the owner of the land. All was in order, however, except that there would be a small legal fee to have the contract made, and we would be expected to share the expense with the seller of the land. This was customary, so we agreed to accept any incidental expenses that might occur.

After an hour in which we freely discussed details, I finally asked, "Since you have had two days to think and pray about what is involved in acquiring and owning land, does anyone foresee any unfavorable situation, condition, or problem that might arise with any of you or with the entire church?" In the silence that followed, the people looked at the floor. In a few minutes, all over the room heads began to shake, indicating that they anticipated no difficulties.

Then I stood and asked Teke to translate carefully for me: "When we left here two days ago, we knew what the Lord wanted us to do about this land purchase," I told them. "We have acquainted Dr. Elson with every detail, and he has approved our intentions. Every missionary working among you is acquainted with the love that the Lord has given us toward you. If we had not been certain of the Lord's leading, we would not have become involved this far." Walking over to where Venancio sat, I reached into my pocket for the 20,000 pesos ($1600.00 U.S.) and handed them to him, as I continued: "Here is the down payment that will make the ground Chapultepec yours. We have less than an hour to get it into the hands of the landowner. May God bless you everyone," and I returned to my seat.

There followed no exclamations of jubilation, no hurrahs or whoops of joy. Instead, all over the room people began to wipe away tears, the expression of emotions too deep for words. Never before had one of these Otomi Christians owned an inch of ground. Tito began speaking very low, with his head bowed. Isabel Sinclair whispered in my ear, "Tito is reciting Psalm 41:1 — 'Blessed is he that considereth the poor: The Lord will deliver him in time of trouble,' and Psalm 112: 5-9 — 'A good man showeth favor, and lendeth: he will guide his affairs with discretion.

'Surely he shall not be moved forever: the righteous shall be in everlasting remembrance.

'He shall not be afraid of evil tidings: his heart is fixed, trusting in the Lord.

'His heart is established, he shall not be afraid, until he see his desire upon his enemies.

'He hath dispersed, he hath given to the poor; his righteousness endureth forever; his horn shall be exalted with honor.' "

This was the first opportunity these Otomi had ever had to become independent men rather than serfs. With simple dignity they expressed their gratitude. Venancio was the first to rise. He came to me, put his arms around me in a loving **abrazo**, and said in Spanish, "Gracias, mi hermano." He went to Vera with the same loving gesture and repeated, "Gracias, mi hermana." So did they all, each one embracing both of us in thanksgiving. Suddenly these people, who had been complete strangers to us two weeks ago, became as our own kin. After a prayer of dismissal, the trustee was sent to make the payment and sign the contract.

As we were sitting at lunch at Dobbs' with those who could attend, a messenger came with word that everything had gone well, that the contract was signed and in force. Then came the time for rejoicing. What a glorious day!

CHAPTER TWELVE
OUR CULTURAL CHANGE

Before we left for Mexico City that afternoon, we took the Sinclairs with us to spend a few minutes with Venancio and his wife Celedonia. Now it was time to laugh and rejoice over the events of the morning. Together we reviewed the purchase of the land and the bright prospects. I said to Don, "Tell Venancio to watch the maturing and ripening of the wheat. When it is ripe and close to being harvested, keep us informed. We will fly down, close the contract, and be with you when you are given possession of the land. We can only be here a few days, but we would like to be present then."

Venancio was pleased. We had prayer together, again in Otomi and English, but each understood the other. Then Venancio and Celedonia gave us warm **abrazos**, with tears in their eyes. We thanked Don and Isabel for their great help to us during the last few days, embraced them, said goodbye and were on our way.

It gave us no little pleasure to bring Ethel Wallis and the Elsons up to date on the situation and our plan to return, probably in early June. Until then, we bade our friends at the Wycliffe headquarters goodbye and went back to pack our car to start north next morning. We went by way of Ixmiquilpan, "our town," rather than by Route 57 as we had planned, pausing only long enough to get a tank of gas, since affairs at home were demanding our attention.

I had taken many pictures of our new missionary project and while sightseeing, so we had much to "show and tell," as well as some kind of gift for just about everybody. But how could we fully explain the adventure into which we had entered in a foreign land?

Winter ended, and the heavy farm work of spring was soon upon us. May passed and June arrived almost before we realized it. The wheat crop on our Indiana farm began to stretch and head beautifully. It was heavy, green, and lush.

During the last week of May we had a long distance call from Mexico. Isabel Sinclair's voice came over the wire. "Laborers are beginning to harvest the wheat," she told us. "Venancio thinks that at the rate they are going, they could be finished by the second day of June."

"We estimated it pretty close," I replied. "I've been working toward that date. In fact, we have reservations to fly June 2, on American Airlines Flight 905, to arrive in Mexico City at 2:30 p.m."

"Good! We'll meet you at the airport," she promised. "Shall we make reservations for you at Dobbs' again?" "Fine," I assented. "Ask for Room No. 7. We'll see you!"

On June 2, thrilled with anticipation, we arrived right on time. As we cruised along, the captain came back through the aisle and sat down beside me for a little visit. He asked, "What takes you two to Mexico?" We told him about our unexpected missionary agriculture project that had started in January, and that the name of our town was Ixmiquilpan, in the state of Hidalgo. He sauntered back up through the cabin, nodding and speaking to passengers. In about fifteen minutes, the stewardess came to our seats and told us, "The captain wants you to come up front." We followed her up to the front of the plane. The captain came out of the cockpit, and pointing out of the right front window, said, "There is your town." Sure enough! — we recognized Ixmiquilpan by the army post on Colony Hill.

Not only were Don and Isabel at the airport to meet us, but when we came through customs and through the door to the public lobby, who should be there with them but Venancio and Tito! Since neither had ever been to an airport before, it was an astounding sight for them to watch as our huge plane arrived.

On the way through the city to the Pan American Highway, we stopped at Wycliffe headquarters long enough for me to cash a check for $3600 into 45,000 pesos. Our pent-up emotions rushed ahead of Isabel's jeep station wagon, but we managed to catch up on three months' news on the way and actually arrived in about the usual length of time. We checked in at the motel, then went to Sinclairs' for supper, and a very brief visit, so anxious were we to be certain of getting up early. I wanted to be sure I missed nothing of watching the end of the wheat harvest.

Don planned to interpret, so the next morning I started bright and early to walk up Colony Hill to his house. In the next three minutes I was to pass through three worlds. On the filling station apron in front of Dobbs' I met a Mexican boy or two and said "Hi!" "Hi!" they responded immediately. Beginning to climb the hill, I met a Mexican man. Again I said, "Hi!" He silently looked up at me and made no reply, so I tried again. "Buenos dias, Senor." He tipped his hat and smiled. "Buenos dias, Senor," he greeted me this time. Still farther up the hill, I met an elderly lady on her way down. I tipped my hat and experimented. "Buenos dias, Senora," I said politely. She lowered her eyes and made no reply. On the next breath, I said, "Hat-si (Good morning)!" She turned quickly, smiled, and approached with her hand outstretched. "Hat-si," she replied pleasantly. Three languages — English, Spanish, and Otomi — in three minutes. I was becoming multilingual.

Don joined me, and we walked to Venancio's house. Tito had already arrived, as had Teofilo and Felipe, so we all walked down to the wheat field where the grain was being harvested. It never occurred to me how the wheat straw would be cut. I, the American farmer, could scarcely believe my eyes when I saw a dozen men lined up with hand-sickles, cutting the standing grain exactly the same way Boaz of Bethlehem harvested it, three generations before King David. The reaper reached with his left hand and grasped the standing wheat a few inches below the heads. He held them upright and taut, as he slid the sickle blade down behind the handful of straw. At about six inches from the ground, he leveled the sickle blade, gave a strong pull, and severed the grain from the ground. Then he laid the handful horizontally on the stubble. He repeated this routine, placing the handful that he had just cut on top of the pile on the ground until there was sufficient for a sheaf, and then he started a new pile. Shortly, another laborer would come along and tie the loose straws of wheat into a sheaf.

We watched as these reapers slowly but surely whittled down the patch of standing grain, until it seemed possible that the work would be finished by the end of the day. This would fulfill the requirements for the final settlement in the time stipulated and would give the Otomi the title to Chapultepec.

Without any thought of the effect on the men at work, I did something that turned out to be as opportune an act as anything I ever did. Quickly I reached down with my left hand to one of the piles of cut grain and grasped a handful right below the heads. With my right hand I divided the straw ends into two parts; then with a fast twist and flick of the wrist, I brought half of the straw up, around, and over the heads in the left hand. Holding the knot in the right hand, I reached over and picked up the rest of the bunch of straw from the ground, and using the spliced straw as a string, I twisted it and tucked it tightly under. As I dropped a firm, solid, tightly-bound sheaf of wheat at the Otomi workers' feet, they let out whoops of joy, like a bunch of schoolboys over a home run. They began talking rapidly to each other, smiling from ear to ear.

Don told me, "They are saying to each other, in pure delight, 'He is, like he said, a farmer and a man of the soil. No one but a farmer would know how to tie a sheaf of wheat like that. He is one of us. He will understand us when we wish to talk to him about our land. Now we know why God sent him to visit us; this now makes him an Otomi farmer.' "

Their words of approval went to my heart, because I had no intention of trying to impress them. I said to Don, "Please interpret for me that when I was a boy growing up on my father's farm, we cut wheat with a horse-drawn binder and later a tractor-drawn binder. Sometimes the twine string which tied the bundles became tangled so it would miss tying the bundle. My father taught me to shock wheat with him, i.e., stand the bundles on end, heads up, leaning toward the center so that the air could dry out the grain for a few days. When we came to an untied bundle, Dad taught me to make a double band of straw and tie the bundle so that the heads would not be scattered and lost, just as I did a few minutes ago. I'm so glad he taught me, because it helps me to become one of you." The reapers finished cutting and binding the field of wheat that day.

The next day, June 4, Venancio and Tito sent word all over the village announcing a special service at the church that night. Everyone possible was expected to be present. That morning I gave to Venancio the 45,000 pesos needed to close the land contract, which he in turn gave to Tito who had been selected to become the trustee for the association.

We mingled with the people who were now preparing for the evening service and walked along the riverbank, beside Chapultepec, which was lined with huge cypress trees, many of which were five and six feet in diameter at the base — trees that must have been old when the United States became a nation — a scene of breathtaking beauty.

Every seat in the church was filled that night, and people were standing. The church orchestra, accompanied on a little portable organ played by Isabel Sinclair, and a choir plus a women's choral group, filled the place with music. The ministers prayed, followed by the announcements and offering. The offering basket had a long wooden handle like an old-fashioned cornpopper. My wife and I were invited to sit on the platform. This was not only an honor, bur a position which commanded a good view of the faces of the people.

Venancio told the congregation for the first time why we were there, and also told them that an association of the church members had become the new owners of a piece of land called Chapultepec, as of that date. He announced that the theme of the service was chosen from Psalm 107, verses 35-37, and he recited it to the people from memory: "He turneth the wilderness into a standing water, and dry ground into watersprings.

"And there he maketh the hungry to dwell, that they may prepare a city for habitation;

"And sow the fields, and plant vineyards, which may yield fruits of increase."

He said that even though the land had been given by Senor Armando and Senora Elvira to an association of eight men, it was given for the benefit of the entire church.

I was invited to the podium to speak. Don Sinclair stood at my left and Venancio at my right. Don translated the things I said into Spanish and Venancio from Spanish to Otomi. I suppose I spoke for fifteen minutes, but by the time it went through Spanish and Otomi, it took most of an hour. I related how the Lord led us to see them and their needs through the eyes of farmers, bringing us to realize that ownership of land would solve some of their needs. Now that we owned the land, we were dedicating it in the Name of the Lord and were now presenting it to the Otomi believers of Colony Hill. This, I explained, was the reason we visited them so frequently and why we came back two days ago. As this was translated to the people in Otomi, Venancio went into great detail. He told how he and Tito had been called into Mexico City in February for advice, of our exacting conferences at Sinclairs' when some of the right men were present, and how the land contract was arranged on February 25th. Finally, he told them how I could bind sheaves of wheat like the harvest laborers, which meant that I knew the language of their hearts.

There was much to be said, and Don fed it back to us in English so that we heard the expression of their gratitude. Then several prayed, and there was more music and congregational singing.

Then Venancio called Vera to the podium, and Don followed at her side. Venancio and Tito presented her with the most beautifully-woven **rebozo** (shawl) we had ever seen. It was black and white wool, with fringe and a design of clusters of grapes and leaves, in a most artistic pattern. There was also a matching bag. It made a priceless gift. It was presented in the name of the church, but Lazara, Tito's wife, had designed and woven it. Vera was both surprised and delighted. She has worn this wrap many times in Mexico and the States. Often we've been seated in restaurants, when strangers have come to our table and remarked, "Your shawl is the most beautiful I have ever seen. Where did you get it, and where can I get one like it?" And Vera always answers — a bit regretfully because they are so disappointed — "Thank you. I too think it is beautiful. It is a gift from our Otomi church at Ixmiquilpan, Mexico. I doubt if there is another like it."

By this time, church would have been dismissed, had we been attending church at home. But instead, a communion service was announced — which brought with it another new experience.

The dictionary says that communion means mutual participation. To the Otomi it meant that the broken bread is passed on a tray, with each one taking a bit, and the mutual participation came with the passing of the grape juice in a single cup. Up to now, we had partaken of the grape juice in tiny gleaming individual glasses or plastic cups. Now we faced a cultural gap that we must cross immediately. We reverently remained quiet in our chairs on the platform, as row after row of the congregation came to the altar, knelt, and were served until the audience of at least a hundred and fifty persons had partaken. Then with the pastor, the assistant pastor, Don and Isabel Sinclair, Vera and I, without hesitation also knelt at the altar and were served from the tray and the mutual cup. Now we had proved to ourselves and to the Otomi that we were one with them, brothers in Christ.

An important occasion such as the acquisition of new land called for a fiesta. So at noon the next day, a church fiesta was held in our honor at the home of Venancio and Celedonia. Very early that morning, the Otomi brethren supervised by Luis, butchered a prime young goat and placed it in a pit on sizzling hot

These two photographs were taken at the Gamio Linguistic Center. They show the believer Otomi brethren in the process of transferring barbeque goat from the ground into tubs to serve a large fiesta gathering. The food is placed on the guest's plate with a bare hand. Note the mounds of sand in the foreground of the bottom fiesta photograph. These mounds conceal more goats.

rocks, covered it with maguey leaves, and buried it under a heap of sand for five hours. In Venancio's courtyard, a separate building had been made into a large, roomy dining area, furnished with homemade tables and benches, its many windows admitting plenty of light and air.

We had never eaten goat meat in the States. Here we faced another new experience — eating a food that had always been low on our totem pole. But when the meal was served, we ate goat meat, served with tortillas, a bit of chili sauce, and rice and broth. We found it appetizing and really delicious. We ate it with love for the Otomi and enjoyed it to the fullest because all Otomi enjoy goat meat. Since then, we have eaten and enjoyed lamb, turkey, and goat — all cooked the same way. Even the Polynesians would relish the food of the Otomi.

But before we finished the meal, an amazing thing happened in this drouth-stricken land. We heard the sound of rain on the roof, as a hard rainstorm began, and hail fell so loudly that we could not hear one another talk. The people laughed with joy and scooped up handfuls of hailstones, because this was the biggest and best rain in years.

The next day was bright and warm. I took Don Sinclair and members of the newly-formed association down to our land near the riverbank for a last conference. All agreed that these two fields were enough for a start. However, if the Lord blessed the project with success, we should look for additional land so that more capable and deserving brothers could also have a chance for full employment. So standing in a circle, we prayed around in turn, asking God to keep His hand upon this new experiment, and if it was His will to supply us more land, to please point it out to us at the right time. Since this was the season for plowing and planting, the Christian men decided that their crop should be two fields of corn.

Adjoining Chapultepec on the right lay a piece of land similar in nature and quality to the one we had just purchased. It lay between the road and the river and was owned by a family by the name of "Honey." Mr. Honey, too, had come to Mexico from the States, married a Mexican girl, and went into the business of farming. The name of the parcel of land adjoining Chapultepec was "La Vina" (the vineyard). It was more than twice the size of the piece we had purchased. We all agreed that day that if La Vina should ever be offered for sale, we would be the logical buyers because of its proximity to Chapultepec.

When we bade the Otomi brethren goodbye, we were all in tears. It was like leaving the family for six months. Accustomed by this time to Mexican **abrazos**, we felt that it was a good way to meet and to part. This time the parting proved more difficult than the first time. Don and Isabel drove us back to Shirley Courts in Mexico City to await our flight back to the States the next afternoon.

As guests at dinner in our hotel dining room that evening we had Dr. Ben and Adelle Elson and Ethel Wallis. We enjoyed updating them on the events of the past few days. Tying in these more recent happenings with those of February made the whole story seem like a fairy tale. Fairy tales do not keep one awake at night, however, nor do they flood one's heart with joy and gratification. We concluded that truly we were generously repaid for heeding a divine compulsion.

CHAPTER THIRTEEN
YOU HAD BETTER BE SINCERE

The following day we flew back to our home in Indiana to resume our responsibilities. We were tempted to relate everywhere the story of our experience with missions, and I did show pictures of events in Mexico to anyone even slightly interested. Most of our friends concluded that, yes, we had an interesting project. But most of them were glad that we instead of they had had the experience. For their part, they were willing to settle for the nice life in the States.

Another normal summer passed, with crops average to good throughout the state. I kept busy in my subdivision enterprise, building streets, installing culverts, side ditches and drains. Building sites sold readily. Occasionally we heard from Mexico and the reports were always good. Pictures of the Otomi brethren harvesting a bountiful crop of corn accompanied one report.

At noon on the first day of November, Isabel Sinclair called from Mexico. She said she was calling for Venancio and Tito concerning the Honey land. "It looks as if the Lord has answered your prayers with the brethren regarding additional land," she told us, "and perhaps earlier than you may have expected. Mr. Honey has been in poor health for sometime, and in midsummer he passed away. They have only one daughter, Mrs. Smith. Neither the Smiths nor Mrs. Honey know how to manage their land, so they have suddenly decided to sell it. They had been told what an excellent job of farming the Otomi believers were doing on their newly-acquired land. Mrs. Honey called Venancio and

Tito to her home, complimented them on the fine appearance of Chapultepec, and asked them if they would like to buy all of her land. They were all speechless and finally asked for a few days to decide. They are here with me, and want to ask your advice."

Now I was speechless, as well. I needed to know more, but in my mind I quickly took an invoice of our resources. We had three kinds of money. We had working money to pay for improvements and street building, money to live on, and some in savings. It was our policy not to allow the Lord's money to accumulate and remain unused for long. In February we had $10,000 in savings. We had used half of it to pay for the Chapultepec land, but the other half was still in savings. I knew Isabel was on a long-distance call, so I began to ask questions and listened carefully to her answers. "How much land does Mrs. Honey have?" I asked. "She has 31 hectares (62 acres) in all," was Isabel's reply. "How many pieces of land are included?" was my next question. "Five pieces of land, including La Vina," she answered. "Where are the other pieces of land located?" Isabel consulted the men and then replied, "El Bondo is on the Pan American Highway near the Tula River bridge; Morales is east of Ixmiquilpan on the road to San Nicolas; San Nicolas adjoins Morales and runs to the edge of the village San Nicolas; the other lies across the road from Morales, and we forget the name of it." "Is it all for sale?" "Yes, all of it." Then I summarized, "That makes five pieces of land with La Vina. Is there anything else?" "There is a plow and a good tractor for sale also," Isabel said.

Trying to itemize it all, I asked, "Can any or all of these things or pieces of ground be purchased separately without the rest?" Isabel answered, "No, she will not divide any part of it; all of the pieces of land and the implements must be sold together."

Then I presented the big question: "How much does she want for it all?" After consultation with Venancio and Tito, she replied, "She priced it to us for 250,000 pesos ($31,250 U.S.). She wants us to have it if we wish, and she is giving us first chance to buy it." Wanting to know further details, I asked, "How does she want the money paid?" "She wants 40,000 pesos ($5,000 U.S.) down and the remainder as we make money from the crops. We can have a deed and clear title for each parcel of land as we pay for it in full," was the reply. "The transaction would be in the form of a contract, and it would draw a small rate of interest each year on the remainder of the amount we would be owing."

"Are there enough men available to tend so much land?" was my next practical question. "Can you operate the tractor and implements successfully and keep them repaired?"

"There are a dozen men who would like to work the land, in addition to the association of eight," was the reassuring reply. "Tito's son is a mechanic who could keep the tractor and implements in good repair."

I had been jotting down questions and answers as fast as I could, while Vera held the notebook and turned pages as needed. Finally I asked, "What do you really wish to do? Are you willing to undertake such a load on faith?" And the Otomi men, through Isabel, reminded me, "Before you left here in June, we prayed together and we felt that we should try to buy La Vina when it was for sale. Now that we will have to buy so much to get it, however, we felt we must tell you and ask your advice."

I turned from the phone and asked Vera what she thought about using the rest of our savings to increase our missionary agricultural project. "Do as you think best," she advised. "Do as you are led to do."

"Isabel, are you still there?" I asked into the mouthpiece.

"I'm still here," she replied. "Where did you go?"

"I was saying a little prayer and counting our money," I quipped. "Ask the brothers, if we furnish the $5,000, do they believe they can manage the land, make it pay for itself, and satisy Mrs. Honey?" In a minute, she reported back: "They are confident they can, and they seem unafraid."

Then I closed the conversation, knowing this call would cost many pesos — "Tell them congratulations! I will put a check in the mail tomorrow for $5,000."

November seemed to fairly drag along, as did December, so impatient were we to get down to Mexico and see what we had acquired. Our January plans were already made, so we closed our year and hurried through with our tax work as fast as possible so we could get away for a month or two.

This time we drove to San Antonio, crossed the border at Laredo, and followed the new, fast Route #57 to Mexico City. We registered at Shirley Courts for an indefinite stay and unpacked for a brief rest and visits with friends we had met last year. In a couple of days we packed an overnight bag or two and drove out to Dobbs' at Ixmiquilpan, asking again for our favorite, Room #7. By now, the folks at Dobbs' knew and liked us in spite of the way we butchered their Spanish. They met our every need, their food was always good, and we enjoyed their cheerful, welcoming smiles every time we stayed there, over the years.

When we knocked on Venancio's gate, he welcomed us with the usual **abrazo** and a beaming smile. Two items had been added to his courtyard that we had not seen last year — one a

(Left to right) Isabel Sinclair; Marge Somerville, a typist; Celedonia, Pastor's wife; Pastor Venancio; and Dr. Donald Sinclair.

Don and Isabel Sinclair

corn crib heaped full of beautiful ears of corn, and the other a tractor, clean and polished, parked by the crib. There was an abundance of news to catch up on, and it was well that the Sinclairs were at hand to serve as interpreters. Impatient to see all the land, we loaded the jeep station wagon. Commencing with Chapultepec, then La Vina and El Bondo, we visited every parcel, learning about its characteristics and possibilities. It was a glorious sight from one end to the other. This purchase had put together a farm operation beyond anything we had ever hoped or planned. It appeared to be flawless in every detail.

CHAPTER FOURTEEN
THEY SHOW THEIR METTLE

A great transformation had taken place in the appearance of the first piece of land we had purchased in February, 1959. The brethren had cleaned the irrigation ditches and installed new cement control gates, making a neat and efficient operation. They had picked up every stone they could find in the fields and used them to raise the height of the rock fence. The standing stalks that bore the crop indicated the health of the ground. The stalks, large and tall, denoted fertile soil. Two giant pecan trees had produced some nuts, a sample of which they had saved for us. It was obvious at a glance that the land was in good hands.

Venancio gathered a group of men to meet with me for a conference lasting a couple of hours, with Don serving as faithful interpreter. First of all, they wished to thank us for getting them possession of the Honey land. Again everyone felt that it was of the Lord, and they mentioned that the believers thanked God each day for His goodness to them through us. They also explained what a delight it was to deal with Mrs. Honey and Mrs. Smith because they both seemed to have confidence in the Otomi brethren. They assured me that although they had allocated land to those who wished to tend it, the members of the association kept their eyes on the over-all operation. Any of the farmers might use the tractor and its operator at an hourly rate. They told me that the ground El Bondo would be rented to a garage owner, since it was in town and located directly on the Pan American Highway. Since late January was the time to plow and prepare the land for spring planting, they were discussing and deciding what crops would be planted in each field. The talk of these men showed sound judgment, and I liked what I heard. There was no doubt but what they would succeed.

In the course of the discussion, I expressed my confidence in Wycliffe Bible Translators and said that as we had become intimately acquainted with Dr. and Mrs. Elson and the Wycliffites who worked among the Otomi, our acquaintance had grown into admiration and trust. "There is no doubt but that the Lord wished us to use some of our means to help you get into the business of farming," I added. "I am proud to see things looking so promising, and I believe you will succeed. I have only one request to make. If Wycliffe should ever have need of any land in this area, they should have the option to buy a portion of what we have in our possession, at a fair price." They thought this was a good idea and gladly granted my request. I had no idea, nor did the brethren, that Wycliffe would ever need or want land near this.

In the course of events during the next day or two, we discussed the need of fertilizing the Honey land, in preparation for the first crop. We estimated the amount needed and the cost, which after some reflection, I decided was too much for them to manage so soon. I told them to buy what was needed and I would pay for it. Perhaps after the first crop, they could easily do it themselves.

We next discussed buying a yoke of oxen. Even though they had a tractor, it could not reach some small patches and difficult corners. They agreed to think about it and when we came out again in two or three weeks, we would talk about it further.

We inquired about some of the little churches where several of the brethren served as pastors. One had four walls and no roof. Another had the walls and the roof but no windows or doors. Still another congregation met outside, along a wall, with no church building at all. Conversations about spiritual progress drew us close to the Otomi people and helped us understand them better. On the next trip we planned to find out more about the churches, the secret of their growth and strength, and what program Venancio had in mind regarding employment for those who were not farmers.

This appeared to be the logical time for me to explain the principles guiding us in providing financial help to acquire land and equipment. All such assistance, past and future, was not to be considered a loan but a gift, entailing no obligation. We had given it freely, without any thought of remuneration. We termed it an investment from which we derived great spiritual blessing. However, we considered it a pleasure to be invited into their conferences as a nonvoting guest, but they need not feel obligated to ask my advice. This declaration pleased them greatly, and I was to be invited to spend many hours with them in planning and policy sessions over the next twelve years. We have established a great relationship, based on mutual respect and Christian love.

The next three-day trip we made to the Mezquital endeared us a little deeper in the hearts of the Otomi, as we visited a few of the little churches tucked away among the cactus. Don and Isabel Sinclair took Venancio with us as often as he could go. At one location called El Olivo, I found out one of his secret formulas for a sound, strong, and thriving evangelical church. El Olivo means "the olive," as you may have surmised — but where were the olive trees? Cactus flourished in every direction

The Pastor Marguerito and his family. There is plenty of room for a parking lot here, but there is nothing to park, not even a horse.

This is El Olivo church, a typical church in a far back place. El Olivo means "The Olive," but there is not an olive tree within 50 miles of here.

around the pretty little desert-stone church building. It had but one door and perhaps four windows, a dirt floor, backless wooden benches, a simple platform containing a pulpit with a white cloth draped across it. There were no lights, and no parking lot, since there wasn't even a horse to park.

Pastor Marguerito invited us into the church, where we sat quietly for a few minutes' meditation. Afterward, as we stood near the Sinclair's car, I asked Venancio, "How do these people who worship here become believers? Does the pastor preach regularly, and the people who live nearby are urged to come and hear the Gospel proclaimed in the hope that sooner or later what they hear will cause them to believe on Jesus? Or at least hear something that will keep them coming?"

"No, indeed," he answered quickly. "No, that isn't the way it works. Instead, one who is not a believer has no right to come into the church. Doesn't the Bible say the church is a body of believers? Why, then, should unbelievers come into the church? Nowhere in the Bible does it say the church is for unbelievers. They have no reason to come." Noting our puzzled expressions, he continued, "This church at El Olivo is a day's walk from Ix-miquilpan, the closest and largest market town in this whole area. The land is so dry that corn, beans, or tomatoes will not grow, so the people must walk to market to buy their needed supplies.

"People going to and from market will travel one, two, or three days, carrying on their backs maguey cactus fiber, charcoal, chickens, or a turkey, and perhaps a fleece of wool to sell that they may buy edibles, oil, clothing, or a sombrero. As night approaches, they look for shelter and something to eat. The believers in this neighborhood make passersby welcome to spend the night in their homes. After they have given their guests food and drink, they begin to inquire about what they believe about God. Soon they come to the question, 'Do you believe that God sent His Son, Jesus Christ, into the world that we may believe in Him to save us from our sins, through His blood at the cross?' If the guest does believe, an hour of fellowship will follow. If he does not believe, the family will witness and preach to the guest all night, if necessary, omitting nothing from what they have learned and experienced. If the guest rejects what he has heard, he may leave ungrateful and angry. If he accepts, he will leave as a happy friend, and he will stop on every trip to and from market, eager to hear more and to learn to pray. Soon the new believer will show a marked change in his appearance, conduct, and conversation. As soon as he has a testimony, he will be eager to tell it, and he will be invited to the church to testify, sing, pray, and worship. The idea is for every believer to become an apostle, using every opportunity to share the Good News. Thus we restrict the membership of the church or congregation to those who believe and have proven it. This is the way that Otomi churches start and grow, the one in Ixmiquilpan and all the little ones like El Olivo."

Then Venancio went a step further. "Suppose a believer willingly does something that is an open sin so that he loses his testimony, but later becomes sorry and penitent. He must go to church every night, sit on the back seat, cannot sing, cannot speak, or cannot pray aloud until he repents, makes right his wrong, sits humbly for a few months until he regains his testimony before his neighbors and the church. Then he will be granted all the privileges of a believer."

As I was standing there listening to Don Sinclair interpret what Venancio was saying in answer to my question, my mind went back to the church where I grew up and where my wife and I belonged and attended when we were a young family. Venancio had just laid out a New Testament pattern with which to compare my church of 1920-1950. We were members and officeholders, so we knew the ins and outs in detail. This comparison revealed a great difference and somewhat startled me. Our church was a good stateside church. We had some fine ministers who preached from the Bible. But we were governed by surveys, canvasses, committees, and boards. Once in awhile we held revival meetings and a few were saved. Most new members came by transfer from some other church. Not one person out of twelve carried his Bible to church. There were visitation campaigns intended to persuade more people to come to Sunday School or church. There were board members who thought it was a good idea to give a man a boys' class to teach, to keep the man interested; to ask a couple to sing in the choir to keep them coming; to ask a man to usher to get him there regularly; or to ask a lady to be chairman of the Social Committee, because everyone liked her. The principal idea was to get and keep them there, that they might be helped. Not many came to prayer meeting. Eventually some of the newcomers became church members and some even became board members. Many nights I returned from a church board meeting to roll and toss all night, reviewing some of the distasteful outcomes of church affairs. And many times I have said to my wife the next morning, "Surely there has to be a better way of running the business of God's Church."

Venancio did not say so, but he showed me that we had been playing church in our younger days. No wonder that it grew very little. It looked as if the songwriter knew about our board meetings when he wrote the phrase, "Oh, what needless pain we bear, all because we do not carry everything to God in prayer." We were not like these Otomi believers who at once became apostles. We had been merely church workers.

The church where we belonged (in 1959) was somewhat different. Almost everyone carried his Bible to church. A personal testimony was required for membership, while much stress and high priority was placed on foreign missions. We are therefore better prepared to measure ourselves against Venancio's high standard for a church.

But the conversation at El Olivo that day pretty much explained why our hearts burned within us that afternoon when Bill Nyman brought us to the Mezquital for the first time. It isn't surprising that we wanted to keep returning whenever possible, to learn more from these fascinating people. It was easy to come to love them dearly. We could not resist helping them to get into the farming business. And we can understand why they have young churches everywhere. They have their priorities straight, and they do not easily change their ways.

CHAPTER FIFTEEN
HOOSIERS AND OXEN AREN'T COMPATIBLE

The next day we suggested to the Otomi brethren that now was a good time to hunt a yoke of oxen that might be for sale. Venancio, Tito and Teofilo could go, but none of the missionaries were available. I said to Vera, "This will be a good time to try out the effectiveness of our cultural change." And that is what we did. We found out, however, that our culture had not changed as much as we thought. I had been farming more than five hundred acres in Indiana, using a full set of implements, including tractors, plows, discs, cultivators, spreaders, combines, a corn and soybean planter, a corn picker, a baler, an elevator — everything that we considered necessary to run a farm. Now I thought it would be fun to buy a yoke of oxen.

Someone had told the Otomi brethren that a Mexican living up in the Queretero area had some oxen for sale. Away we went — two **gringos** in the front seat and three bilingual Otomi (bilingual only in Otomi and Spanish, but not English) in the back. Queretero was some 70 miles away, and we were hunting **dos** toros (two bulls). We navigated by the directions: **adelante** (straight ahead); **a la derecha** (to the right); **a la izquierda** (to the left); and **alto aquí** (stop here). It turned out to be quite a lark. We did not buy any **toros**, but we had fun with the brethren and they had fun with us. It turned out that the man only had one bull for sale; he was a good animal but too expensive, and no one knew where we could find a teammate for him. We did manage to get an estimate that a good matched team, well-broken, would cost about 5,000 pesos ($400.00 U.S.). A few days later, someone gave the men information as to where they could find some oxen, so we gave them the money and told them to buy the best they could. When we came out on the next trip, they had their oxen.

One day I said to Don Sinclair, "Do the Otomi mothers sing to their babies to quiet them and get them to sleep?" Don replied, "I have never heard one sing to her child." I had observed that the children were quiet and happy as a rule. But I probed further. "Surely once in awhile a child needs special attention. What would she say?" Don answered that she would say, "S-s-s-s-s-s-s-s-s, S-s-s-s-s-s-s-s-s."

Just a few days later, the brethren wanted me to try my hand at plowing with the oxen. The plow was a single-handle, wooden beam, single shovel, hitched to the yoke, far more primitive than the horse-drawn plow with a steel beam and moldboard, having two handles — like the one I plowed with when I was a kid. Bravely, I stepped behind the plow and took the handle in my right hand. There were no lines to guide the oxen or a goad to start them. I looked at Don and said, "Ask them what I say to start these guys moving." He did, and they answered, "S-s-s-s-s-s-s-s-s, S-s-s-s-s-s-s-s-s." I must have said, "S-s-s-s-s-s-s-s-s, S-s-s-s-s-s-s-s-s," in good Otomi, because they took off at a lively gait, dragging me with them, and I plowed the crookedest furrow anyone ever saw. I jumped from one side to the other, trying to guide the plow, but nothing helped. My great-grandfather would have been ashamed of me, but the Otomi thought it was a great exhibition. They howled with laughter.

When I came to the end of the field, I didn't know what to do. I had forgotten to ask what to say to stop them. Someone called out something which I didn't understand — but the oxen did. They came to an immediate halt. Well, I didn't do any worse than the brethren expected, and they loved me for trying.

Before we returned to Mexico City, we again discussed with Venancio and Tito the needs of some of the small surrounding churches. It gets cold in the Valley during December and January. For that reason, the Mexican schools along the highways do not open until February. We decided to put a door and windows in one church and the roof on another. It took 1,250 pesos ($100 U.S.) for each church, to make them weatherproof. On the mission field, again so little does so much.

At Wycliffe headquarters we heard that Nancy Lanier at Tetzu had a new partner in her translation work. Her name was Patricia Cowan, another single girl, a newcomer to Mexico — and this was her first assignment. On our next trip to the Mezquital, we drove up to Tetzu to visit the girls.

The water situation had deteriorated until the girls would fill the wash pan half-full each morning, and then both would wash their hands in it all day. They set the dishwater back on the stove and washed the dishes from their three meals in it.

Since Pat Cowan knew very little of either Spanish or Otomi, she performed the more menial tasks of the household and freed Nancy to spend her time at her desk working on the translation with her language helper. Thus Pat spent her day cooking, washing dishes, buying eggs, etc., from Otomi neighbors, selling kerosene to meet the needs, visiting in the neighborhood to master the language, showing women new patterns for their weaving, telling the children Bible stories with the aid of the flannelgraph, selling rebozos (shawls) made by Otomi women to buyers in Mexico City, and carrying water from the cement storage tank which served the village from its location half a mile away. Part of the time it was empty. All this activity helped her to make friends with the people, however, and to become acquainted with their culture. Soon she had a grasp of the language, and the people loved her for it. Her willing service in the household was invaluable to both of the team.

Just the day before we arrived, Pat had fallen as she carried two buckets of water home, and her knees had been badly cut and bruised by the jagged stones in her path. The girls had acquired a frisky dog named Thrombo. He darted in front of Pat and tripped her so that she fell. This was reason enough for me to design a new water system. I ordered a steel drum to be anchored onto a flat wooden platform on the roof of the house. Through the bottom of the tank we brought a water pipe down beside a partition wall into the house. We connected it to a shower stall, a bathroom lavatory, and the kitchen sink. On the ground beside the house, we anchored a hand-operated water pump. A hose was attached to the pump, taken straight up past the edge of the roof, and fastened securely to the steel drum. We gave the girls some money to be set aside as a water fund, with which they were to hire an available Otomi boy to keep water in the drum at all times. The water was easily available by gravity, and the sun would warm it for a shower, the lavatory and the kitchen sink. It could be boiled for drinking, dishwashing, and rinsing. The boy could easily and quickly pump buckets of water into the supply tank, and he would no doubt be delighted to earn a few pesos a week.

Talk about two happy girls! — and we had accomplished this with a minimum of effort and expense. There are scores of such simple tasks that laymen can do on anybody's mission field, if they will only volunteer their services. And it is a joy to get involved this way.

The first two months of 1960 passed quickly. We enjoyed the comforts of Shirley Courts, where we made new friends and enjoyed the ones we had met the year before. We soon publicized our heart interest in the Mezquital Valley and enjoyed a number of opportunities to take friends there for short visits.

Typical street scene in the village of Tetzu. There may be two or three streets that one can carefully drive a car or Jeep through with a bit of maneuvering.

Street scene in the village of Tetzu.

Tía Melisia (Aunt Melissa), sitting at the door of her tiny organ cactus home. She was desperately poor, very deaf, spoke Otomi only, and had been out of her environment only once for a one week visit with her sister in Mexico City. She became our warm and lovely friend. When there was no interpreter present, we communicated by signs, gestures, smiles, gifts and we understood each other. She earned five pesos (.40¢ U.S.) every two weeks carding wool for a neighbor.

Tia Melisia was not a believer, mostly because she could not hear or understand. One day the Sinclairs and we visited her, and Isabel Sinclair set up an appropriate flannel-graph. Over and over Isabel showed and told her the Gospel story by loudly repeating the message in her ear.

Isabel Sinclair prayed for her and we believe that Tia Melisia became a believer in Christ as her Saviour that day. Only a few months later, neighbors found her dying in her home all alone. We greatly grieved her passing, but rejoice that she showed a marked change after she said she believed.

Tia Melisia and Author. It gets cold here, so a new blue sweater was severely needed.

Nancy Lanier and Pat Cowan live in Tetzu in this house that Ethel Wallis built when she first was assigned to work among the Otomi. This is about 12 miles north of Colony Hill. We installed a simple water system on the housetop.

These are the water boys who carried water and pumped it to the roof top tank on Nancy and Pat's home. They made a little money and the girls enjoyed the luxury.

Nancy (left) and Pat (right) standing in their front yard visiting with Amalia and baby.

This is Amalia, a beautiful and photogenic Otomi wife with her child. The baby is being typically carried on its mother's back, happy and secure in a rebozo. Amalia is especially talented in weaving.

Patricia Cowan, the junior partner of Nancy Lanier, is teaching Otomi children at night by kerosene lamp on the porch. Otomi children love being taught by flannel-graph and quickly learn to read and sing.

CHAPTER SIXTEEN

WE BEGIN TO BRANCH OUT

Mexico City proved to be a great place to vacation and a fascinating city in which to live. We began using taxis to go downtown, to the Zocolo, to church, to the markets, and the famous Chapultepec Park. For three pesos we could ride to Wycliffe headquarters where we attended both Sunday and Wednesday night services. We soon became better acquainted and were invited to enjoy other occasions, as well. We learned about Jungle Camp, located in the State of Chiapas near the Guatemala border, where Wycliffe trains their new recruits in survival methods under primitive conditions. We accepted an invitation to go down there for a week, and could not believe the world into which we had moved. To say that I returned nine times in ten years will tell you something of its fascination. My wife, as well as a number of guests, shared in several of these trips.

In fact, we found ourselves learning the whole story of Wycliffe's many facets so rapidly that sometimes we couldn't remember it all. We heard missionary stories such as we had dreamed they should be. In a single year we had personally become acquainted with over a hundred missionaries. In some ways they seemed alike, but their reports of varied experiences in differing cultures never ceased to fascinate us. No two stories were alike. We often asked ourselves, "Why haven't we heard of these people before? Why did we have to come to Mexico to hear about Wycliffe Bible Translators? Surely someone should be telling Hoosiers about such a group."

Director Ben Elson and his wife Adelle began inviting us to their apartment for a meal or a snack, and I was often invited to his office. We in turn entertained the Elsons and others for lunch or dinner at Shirley Courts and visited together afterwards in our room. Occasionally we took half a dozen single girls to the Pom Pom Restaurant for after-service refreshment on Sunday evenings. Nearly every Sunday, too, we invited a missionary or two for the noon meal and would introduce them to tourist friends from the States. We enjoyed times of rich fellowship with these missionaries, and we formed deep and lasting friendships with many of them.

As I recall, this was the year that I felt a strong desire to see Guatemala and visit Wycliffe's work there. So shortly before time to go back to Indiana to take up the summer's work, I suggested this to Vera. She didn't want to go, however, and I invited Ben Elson to be my guest for a few days in Central America.

From the moment we arrived until the day we left, this jaunt was a well-planned, exciting experience. Guatemala is about the size of Ohio, but most of it stands on end like a miniature Switzerland with mountains and volcanoes. The weather was perfect for traveling all over the place by plane and carryall. In remote places we visited strange peoples. We saw teams working where miracles which resulted from Bible translation had transformed the lives of the people. Reluctantly we left, but I promised to return and bring my wife the next time. Guatemala's mission fields were full of opportunities for laymen to help with essential projects. It proved to be a photographer's paradise, as well.

Since returning to Indiana from Mexico in 1959, I have shown my pictures and told the story of pioneer missions in general, and Wycliffe Bible Translators in particular, in every place I have had opportunity. I decided that it was shameful that we had to go to Mexico to hear the Wycliffe story, and I would do what I could to remedy this situation in my area. Also I felt that other mission-minded people might be glad to learn how they might use some of God's money in a practical way. I had witnessed for myself what a large portion of money given to Wycliffe reached the field, with a minimum diverted into administration. I was glad to tell about it, and my audiences were glad to hear it.

In late autumn, I received a letter from the Board of Wycliffe Bible Translators, headquartered in Santa Ana, California, inviting me to become their official representative in Indiana. Six months later, in May, 1961, I attended my first Corporation Conference of Wycliffe Bible Translators and the Summer Institute of Linguistics, held in Sulphur Springs, Arkansas. During that week I wrote the Board a letter of acceptance and dropped it in their

Conference mail box. That summer and fall my suitcase was never completely unpacked, as I crisscrossed up and down the state telling Hoosiers the Wycliffe story and hunting recruits for the mission field. I saw the need for large central gatherings, so I inaugurated a series of annual Wycliffe dinner rallies which were held in Indianapolis for eight consecutive years thereafter. I brought the best Wycliffe talent to that platform with a captivating theme each year, and the rallies were consistently well attended. Some people didn't miss a single meeting.

As some of these experiences we were having caused us to examine our daily habits, Vera and I became aware and ashamed of the way we were neglecting our Bibles. We had read and reread the familiar parts — the 23rd Psalm, the Story of Creation, the Flood, stories of Joseph, David, Daniel, of Jesus and His miracles, the Sermon on the Mount, the missionary journeys of Paul, all the interesting parts that are familiar to most Christians. But these were the things we had known since we were kids, "milk" and not "strong meat." Since we had known the Otomi and other people who had never had a Bible in their own tongue, since we had observed closely what was being accomplished by the translators in giving a Living Word to these peoples, we decided now it was time to mend our ways. We began to read our Bibles, together aloud, first thing after breakfast each day. We finished reading it through from Genesis 1 through Revelation 22 for the first time on May 6, 1961. Since that time, we have continued to read it together, until now we have finished reading the Bible in entirety for the 19th time. At first it took us about a year to complete a thorough reading, but now it takes about ten months. Our Bibles are marked from start to finish.

Even yet there are many things we do not understand, but we believe it all by faith, and we find new things to underscore in each reading. We are glad that we decided if the Bible was so essential to pagan peoples, it certainly should be vital to us, in its entirety. What good is a Bible to a person, especially a believer, if he does not know what it says, we asked ourselves.

When we once again arrived back in Mexico in January, 1961, our first desire was to visit the Otomi farms. There was activity on Chapultepec, La Vina, El Bondo, Morales, San Nicolas, and the rest. Men were busy everywhere. The harvest of the previous year had been bountiful, and heaping corncribs were standing close to many of the houses. Instead of eight interested and busy men, there were now nineteen. Everything was spic and span, as they proudly showed us the results of their labors.

I told Venancio and Tito, "Every place we go, the brothers

are as busy as beavers. Things look so well cared for, and the people seem happy."

Don Sinclair told them what I said, and there was no response. Don said to me, "It rains here usually only once a year, and most of the time far less. For years the people didn't have water enough to take a bath. I don't think they know what a beaver is."

I tried again, "Every place we go, the brothers are as busy as ants. Things look so well cared for, and the people seem happy." That did it. Venancio and Tito smiled and nodded. They really laughed when Don tried to tell them what a beaver was.

That winter I began conducting tours for church leaders and businessmen to the mission fields of Mexico and Guatemala — tours lasting from one to two weeks, depending on the itinerary. I was doing this in hopes that the same exciting experiences might affect others in much the same way as Vera and I were affected in 1959. Almost always I would end my Mexico tours with two days in the Mezquital — without exception, the highlight of the trips.

Guatemala is a beautiful country, full of interesting surprises and a delightful place to take guests. The Guatemala tour that year was over a period of 14 days and nights, profitable and memorable, deluxe in every way. It had been arranged and directed by Ray and Helen Elliott, Marvin and Marilyn Mayers, and Walt and Marilyn Agee.

We were transported all over the country in two or three carryalls, and the days were full of pleasantry. My group was exposed to missions most effectually, and some of my group found projects that especially interested them. Everyone made lasting friendships. We visited strange and different tribal peoples, indigenous churches where they were available, and the missionary couples who worked in the tribes. Some of the highlights of the trip were overnight stays in missionary homes located in storybook settings. I took my wife that year, as I had promised my missionary friends the year before, plus a group of eight from several states and of several vocations.

In the course of a few years, I conducted mission field and Jungle Camp tours for more than twenty-five men and women. Some were very outstanding people and so appreciative that even now, fifteen years later, they occasionally call or write to thank me for making possible such exciting and important experiences.

Ben Elson shared with me from time to time his growing belief that Wycliffe needed two linguistic centers in Mexico, a place where missionary families and their language helpers could gather for three-month workshops. A small center had been established in Mitla, several hundred miles south of Mexico City, but facilities were too limited for efficiency. It seemed to him and to his advisors that a larger site for a translation center should be selected north of Mexico City, perhaps as far north as Ixmiquilpan or Tasquillo. The executive committee was commissioned to find an acceptable place, and they invited me to accompany them.

Available at the outskirts of Tasquillo was a tract of two hectares (four acres), which was in many ways a perfect setting. Water and electricity were available, a blacktop road led to it, a dirt road surrounded it, and it was high ground covered with the most beautiful cactus of every variety in Mexico. It had an unobstructed view of Mt. Juarez, named for the George Washington of Mexico. I fell in love with the place and would have liked nothing better than to own it myself. The price was right, and everything seemed favorable for its purchase as a workshop site.

But when the owners found that Evangelicals wanted to buy it, the price immediately tripled. There we were, wanting a piece of land we could never afford to buy. Missionaries see things like that happening all over the world, but just because there are disappointments, they do not despair, remembering that "all things work together for good to them that love God . . . who are the called according to His purpose."

Recalling my agreement with the Colony believers when we acquired the Honey land, I remarked to the committee, "The last land that we helped the believers buy had several fields. Some of them lay a mile or less east of Ixmiquilpan, on the San Nicolas road. As we were negotiating the deal, I asked that if Wycliffe Bible Translators ever wished to buy a reasonable portion of it, they should have the opportunity to buy it at the price that had been set by Mrs. Honey. The Association, however, must be in unanimous agreement. Since the plot called Morales, which contains about two and a half hectares (5 acres), is on the way back to Mexico City, it might be worthwhile for you to go see it. If I remember correctly, the price is set at around 25,000 pesos ($2,000 U.S.)."

There was nothing to lose and everything to gain, so we drove out of Ixmiquilpan on the San Nicolas road to look at the property. Fifteen minutes after we walked up into the center of Morales, every member of that Executive Committee knew that this was the natural site for what was to become "Gamio Centro de Linguistico," and they said so. They bowed their heads and prayed around the circle regarding it, and then we drove back to Mexico City.

Within days, the Executive Committee approached the Otomi Land Association regarding the purchase of Morales. The Otomi felt that such a center would benefit their people as well as the town, and also Wycliffe, their best friends. They were willing to sell, the price was verified and agreed upon, and legal proceedings were instituted and handled by a Christian Mexican lawyer in the City. At the appointed time, Vera and I gave to Wycliffe the amount necessary to acquire Morales, where it was estimated that a translation workshop would cut the time required to produce a New Testament by fifteen years. Gamio carefully planned and built to serve as the first and most important translation center in the world. It has been used by and has benefited linguists from around the globe.

CHAPTER SEVENTEEN
THE OTOMIS' FINEST HOUR

The sale of Morales and one other field of land gave the believers cash in hand to reduce their responsibility in their contract with Mrs. Honey. There were at least a dozen and a half of the brethren diligently planting, tending, and harvesting one crop after another. I saw a field of wheat they raised and estimated it to yield 50 bushels per acre. At one time they had a field or two in alfalfa, and with consistent irrigation, they cut eight and nine cuttings per year. It was sold green and fresh from the field to be dehydrated and made into pellets, on its way to retail feed stores. Once they had a very large crop of tomatoes. The price dropped so low, however, that there was no market for them. The people didn't make any money on their tomatoes, but they ate so many it was a long time before they wanted to see any more.

El Bondo, on the highway, was bringing in rent. Corncribs were never empty. The poor were being fed. People in the back country were learning to eat carrots and cabbage, and many families were enjoying better health. It was not uncommon for neighbors and fellow townspeople who had formerly mocked the believers because of their faith to stop them on the streets or roads now to compliment them on their prosperous looking fields. Each visit and business conference brought forth more delightful reports. Our prayer of gratitude each day was, "Thank you, Lord, for honoring the Otomi."

One day in early 1962, during our annual trip to Mexico, as

94

we visited the people, the fields, the church and the surrounding area where the believers lived, we discovered new and interesting projects in progress. Competent leaders were conducting reading classes, singing classes, and Bible classes. Isabel Sinclair taught a women's reading class at 6:00 a.m., before they went to the village mill to get their tortilla corn ground. The attendance was so large that if half-filled the church each morning, sometimes as many as 90 women.

With everything progressing as well, we felt we should compliment the members of the Association at the first opportunity. In a few days we were invited to attend a meeting, and I was asked to speak. I felt led to talk at some length. "It is three years now since the Lord sent us to you," I began. "He gave us a vague conception of what you could do if only you had an opportunity. It became clear that the best opening for you would be to own some irrigation land. That conception proved to be of God, and already you have exceeded our expectations. And rather than weakening your testimony, this successful experience has strengthened and broadened it. Already you have become missionaries — and you have just started.

"The Lord has not only blessed you — He has blessed us even more, as we have observed this miracle. You have been wise and capable, and God has prospered you in all your ways. We have observed you closely, and you have taught us many things. You appear to be sound in your judgment and strong in your will. We do not doubt that the Lord will lead you into the riches of His blessing."

When this had been interpreted, I continued, "As we have traveled, we have seen and heard about worthy projects in Southern Mexico, Guatemala, South America, Papua New Guinea, and many other places that need someone to become interested in helping them. Do you believe now that you are financially able to manage your land without further assistance? Do you think it is time for us to look elsewhere for others to help?" As soon as this was interpreted, there were nodding heads all over the group. These were the leaders, and they were agreeing that their financial affairs had reached the place where they would no longer need help.

Tito and Venancio conversed together for a few minutes. Then Tito spoke first. "You have helped us to become strong enough to stand by ourselves. Furthermore, we ourselves can and should be doing more to help others."

Then Venancio spoke, "I have been making several trips up into the mountain area to help new believers to become established," he told us. "In several places we have helped to establish churches in homes and to construct new church buildings. Yes, you have helped us long enough, and we are obligated to help others now."

I think this was the finest hour for the Otomi of the Mezquital. It was a notable turning point in their lives. At this meeting, they shifted into high gear. In fact, they took on a new dignity, a new authority, a new poise. This is when they really commenced to be, as I call them, the "amazing Otomi."

CHAPTER EIGHTEEN
CURIOSITY LEADS ONE TO STRANGE CONCLUSIONS

I got my appetite whetted in the Mezquital Valley through thrilling experiences with the Otomi and being a curious, observant layman, I began pondering over some of the puzzling questions that had been bugging me since 1952.

The first of them was: "Why wasn't this business of getting the Gospel to the ends of the earth, to every tribe and tongue finished years and years ago?"

Another was: "Why is it an established fact that since the invention of the printing press, 28% of everything printed has been in the English language, when only 9% of the world's population speaks English?"

Furthermore: "Why are there nearly 600 versions of the Holy Scriptures printed in English, when almost 4,000 languages spoken in the world do not have one book of the Bible — thousands with not a single verse?" These are honest questions that deserve an answer.

Since the Lord commanded clearly in the Bible several times that the Gospel should be shared, who gives us the right to be so complacent about such inconsistencies? It seems to me that many are going to have to shoulder responsibilities for such ridiculous delays. It appears that it is long past due for all of God's people everywhere to examine their hearts for the cause of their indifference.

It is the goodness of divine providence that we were born in an English-speaking nation. We might have been born in Calcutta, India, or along the Marañon River in Peruvian jungles, in Indonesia, or in a house on stilts on the Island of Jolo in the Sulu

Archipelago. Isn't it time for every Christian layman, pastor, evangelist, seminary professor, and Bible student to roll up his sleeves and get busy? I have never known of a people who did not want or have a god of some sort. People just cannot get along without outside help, and they will accept many substitutes, if they are troubled in their souls. As a last resort, they will even create their own gods.

Using our experiences with the Otomi believers as a testimony of what a pagan people can become when they know the true God, we used it as a springboard to explore for ourselves what it really is like to be without God and without hope. I remember very well where it led us in our thinking and response. Since the things that the eye sees are more convincing than the things the ear hears, there are many strange heart-touching sights we have come upon that might also give you a spiritual shock and a challenge as well. And you might startle yourselves by your response.

It would be a familiar sound, if you were in a small Indian village in the State of Oaxaca, Mexico, high in the mountains, to suddenly hear a homemade bamboo flute whistling a queer tune. It grows louder, and soon you see that it is a family procession, led by the eldest son with the noisy flute. Directly behind him comes the father carrying the family patron saint who has become dreadfully negligent in answering the prayers of this needy group. Behind the father marches the pregnant mother, carrying a small child and leading another, followed by three other older children a year apart in size.

Their mission is to the village church where the itinerant priest is present only on each Wednesday, and the purpose is to have the patron saint recharged to cure his delinquent interest and renew his waning strength. Fees must be paid for this service, so the impoverished father and mother have scraped up every peso and centavo in the house and tucked them deep under their poncho or rebozo.

After the priest was convinced that nine pesos was all the father had, he performed the ritual, took the nine pesos, and sent the little family on their way home with relieved hearts. The priest had not asked about the four pesos and seventy centavos which the mother had tucked away in her blouse.

The parade home was better because the flute tune was livelier and louder, especially after they stopped at the roadside liquor vendor's jug and spent the four pesos and the seventy centavos for refreshments for all, to celebrate the prospects of a better life — until their patron saint runs down again, like a spring-wound toy. Isn't it a pitiful picture? Aren't you glad that you don't have to depend upon this approach to your God?

A couple of states to the south and east is Chiapas, the state which borders the country of Guatemala. From the city of San Cristobal Las Casas it is only a short jungle-plane ride to Lacandone country, where we will land on a bumpy grassy landing strip called Naja. It is commonly agreed by anthropologists that the Lacandone people have the purest Mayan blood in the world. To reach the village of Naja, we must be poled on a mahogany dugout canoe across a lagoon lake thickly infested with alligators. A Lacandone man is our guide and provides the horsepower. He wears an ankle-length, woven dress of burlap-textured material, stiff with dirt and filth, which blends in with his waist-length matted and tangled hair. Upon reaching the village shore, the first person you meet is Chief Mateo. The Chief is a polygamist, and following him are two or three sets of children and grandchildren from the ages of one to twenty. The Chief and those following are clothed like the man who piloted us to the village. Distinction between the sexes is indicated only by the beads and earrings worn by the women and girls.

Since I have been here perhaps a dozen times before and am acquainted with the Chief, we will soon get to the subject of his gods and his god-house where they are made and worshipped. You may see the god-house and the nine figures seated prominently on the shelf — but you will not be invited to step inside. After seven or eight visits, I was allowed to step inside four steps and take a flashlight picture of the Chief's gods. I was permitted this honor only because I asked to have his picture taken beside them. They were clay gods, fashioned and carefully burned, having heads with eyes, ears, noses, mouths, and chins — and yet they are powerless to think, see, hear, smell, speak, or feel. I know because I have one sitting on my filing cabinet in my Indianapolis office, and he hasn't spoken yet.

The open body cavity of the figures is filled with pitch-pine chips which are lighted, after the figures are lined up in their proper places for worship on the clay floor. During prayer time, the Chief is drunk with liquor and stupefied by added herbs to cause hallucinations so that he may properly address his gods through the evil spirits. Chief Mateo says he prays to the evil spirits, because the good spirits do not give him any trouble. Many of the gods become dilatory and disobedient, so they meet a tragic death by being slammed against a tree trunk, after getting a bitter cursing.

Would you like the Chief to pray for you? He will not, because he is too troubled with his own problems and fears. I once heard him say that his gods did him no good, but he must keep them because his fathers handed down to him the first set of figures and the pattern for making them (Psalm 115:1-9).

Northwest of Guatemala City fifty or sixty miles is a town named Chichicastenango. In the heart of tribal Indian country, it is considered one of the most picturesque in Guatemala, especially on a market day and on a few other special days. The colorful **rebozos,** blouses, and skirts of the women and children, contrasted with their raven-black hair, make a mammoth kaleidoscope, as they mill and mingle to and fro through the narrow streets. Market day is special, but routine. No day in Chichicastenango is so important as the second Friday of Lent. On that Friday the patron saint of the town is carried from his resting place in his sacred room, through designated streets which have had fresh pine needles strewn on them the night before. The parade lasts for an hour or more, then ends where it began — at the saint's permanent resting place.

The particular thing that makes Chichicastenango famous, however, (or perhaps the word should be "infamous") is the prevalence of witch doctors. The town is a hotbed of witchcraft in Guatemala. At one time I counted 94 witch doctors in an ancient church on Market Square, performing "costumbre" and other traditional rituals, as a service to their private Indian clientele. It is well understood that no such service is performed without charge — and prepaid. Witchcraft is a horrifying practice, strong and encompassing — a giant net that entangles poor, ignorant people, and from which there is no escape without divine intervention. Witch doctors are the most brazen, overbearing, heartless instruments of the Devil one can find anywhere. They thrive and flourish in Guatemala beyond imagination.

The carrying of the patron saint is such a service of prestige and coveted honor that witch doctors are not only willing to do this without remuneration, but they will even **pay** cash in pesos for the privilege. In fact, this service confers such distinction that no one set of bearers is permitted to go the whole course. At certain points, the procession halts, another set of carriers pays the designated fees and takes their places under the load. I believe each set consists of a dozen men bearing the ornate and cumbersome carriage upon their shoulders. The last set of bearers is probably composed of the very wealthy, because they are formally dressed in navy blue suits with wide red capes to denote their status. No doubt these men are subject to a much larger fee, even if they do not have so far to go. In addition, they are led by a uniformed band of musicians playing loudly, and are engulfed in dense clouds of incense. It is a spectacular sight to witness, and it creates an atmosphere of intense emotion and outcry among the throng of followers and onlookers.

One time I stood on the top steps of the stairs leading up to the resting place and final destination of the saint, and along with a photographer friend from New Hampshire, snapped clear and bright pictures from a distance of six feet, of this heathen god, through the gold-framed windows of his royal carriage as it was borne on the shoulders of some of the most prominent witch doctors of the heathen world. What was he like? The saint was an effigy of a prostrate, broken, and emaciated Christ, with the brown color of the Mayan race. He wore a crown of thorns to portray his suffering and shame. My Christ and Saviour was resurrected from the dead, ascended into Heaven, and lives sitting on the right hand of God, interceding for you and me. Aren't you glad that you do not have to depend on an effigy for your salvation (Exodus 20:3-9)?

We have all heard it said, "All's well that ends well." Despite all the bad news from pagan lands, once in awhile someting good and encouraging comes to our attention to warm the heart and delight the soul. Let's return to Mexico for a current story about Richard and Patricia (Cowan) Beller, Wycliffe Bible Translators who are translating two dialects of the Aztec language. These dialects are distinctly different and both necessary. The Bellers work at them simultaneously for the two separated areas, a difficult task, requiring much patience, working long hours and enduring routine hardships. They have also faced discouragements such as vandalism and theft of medical supplies at the clinic during their absence from the village where they have built their home. They experience further difficulties when the rainy season comes, making their house almost inaccessible. The rivers flood the valleys bringing great mudslides, and both supplies and people must transfer to boats. Then the cargo finished the trip on the backs of villagers. But to Dick and Pat it is all worthwhile, as they look toward the day when these two villages will have the Good News from God, the New Testaments, in their languages.

The Bellers' home village is some 75 miles north of Mexico City, but speakers of the second dialect live farther north. A question often asked is, "After these New Testaments are made available to the people, do they read and use them?" The answer is "Translated portions are usually read and studied while New Testament translation progresses. Some New Testaments are read as soon as they are completed, while in other groups, the people must become proficient readers in order to study them. Sometimes they are taped and played on cassettes to the people of a particular language group. In the village where the Bellers live and operate their clinic, there is an unusually good reason to believe that the Scriptures will be much used."

As soon as Dick and Pat chose a home site, built a clinic, found a language helper, and commenced translation, opposition soon arose. In almost every tribal village, one figure stands out prominently as antagonistic to the new teaching, and often begins to domineer. The Bellers' village ran true to form, since the dominant figure was against everything except motherhood and high taxes, as we sometimes say. Those people who frequented the clinic for medical help were received with kindness, examined, treated, and encouraged, so they left with expressions of gratitude and praise for the translators. Since news passes quickly by word of mouth, daily visitors increased and friendships formed and developed.

Since the village leading citizen had been receiving attention and recognition, he was well satisfied with the status quo. But increasing rumors of the success of these **gringos** living on the edge of town began to meet his outspoken criticisms, in his effort to restore his waning influence.

The Bellers realized the presence of growing opposition, but because they had a mandate, an assignment, and a job to do, they diligently pursued their task. They continued to pray and work, made friends, helped people, learned to speak the language, gained the confidence of the Aztecs, watched their children win the hearts of the villagers, and began to translate their first verses of Scripture.

It wasn't long before the critical and somewhat envious one became curious and sought to learn from the villagers what these Americans were really up to. Few of his Indian friends joined him in his skepticism, so he quieted down.

Experience has taught me that the Lord has a standard procedure of coming into a situation at just the right time. It wasn't long before Troublesome Townsman No. 1 grew bold enough to come see for himself what these newcomers were about. He found them much better and pleasanter than he expected— very likable, in fact. They even spoke pretty good market language, and they showed him what bits of the Aztec language looked like on paper. In spite of himself and his doubts, he liked what he heard and saw. Each visit became a little easier to make and more enjoyable, so he just kept coming and felt at ease.

As soon as complete Bible verses were translated, then chapters, and finally books were printed, the Bellers began to lay them side by side with the same Scriptures in Spanish. Being bilingual readers, the Bellers began reading them to visitors in this man's presence. The result — he turned from a skeptical foe into a warm friend. He readily saw how much more sensible it was for Aztecs to read the Scriptures in their own language, rather than trying to teach them to understand the Scriptures written in Spanish, a language which few of them spoke. He hardly knew what was happening to him, but since many Aztecs were becoming interested in the Aztec Scriptures, some were becoming believers, and these changed lives were something he had never before witnessed.

What do you suppose happened to this "doubting Thomas," who was such an obstinate "die-hard?" Why he became the ray of sunshine which broke through the darkness to warm the hearts of translators and new believers alike. The Lord didn't stop his noisy chatter — He just changed its tone and used it for His glory.

Now, just as soon and just as often as the Bellers finish a portion of Scripture translation, get it printed and ready for distribution, this dear brother gathers up all the copies that can be spared and hurries to the most prominent corner of town each market day. Standing on this advantageous spot, much like a County Fair sideshow barker, he waves portions of Scripture above his head and calls out loud and clear: "Buy the Holy Scriptures; read the Holy Scriptures; believe the Holy Scriptures; obey the Holy Scriptures!"

CHAPTER NINETEEN
I REPRESENT WHAT I BELIEVE

Further travels and additions to our list of missionary friends did not serve to weaken our relationship nor wean us away from our dear friends in the Mezquital. I continued to be invited into the policy-making conferences of the land association. At one time we made a trip to Mexico primarily that I might meet with Venancio and Tito a couple of times to help them work out a plan whereby the land should be deeded to individuals rather than the association. It appeared that the Mexican Government had begun to frown on the idea of groups and associations holding deeds. So to this day we remain warm friends of many Mezquital families. We have even been told that we have some namesakes. In Villa Gran, about ten miles south of Ixmiquilpan, two children were born into two families of Otomi believers. The children are first cousins, about four years old at the time of this writing. One is named Armando and the other Elvira. We first saw them when they were two years old, and we wanted very much to have our pictures taken holding them in our arms. This didn't go over very big with the children, and we finally settled on a lopsided compromise wherein the mothers held the children while we stood at a safe distance. However, we believe we can close this culture gap, next time we go, with a doll and a red dump truck.

Through the years we have taken Stateside friends into the homes of Otomi friends, not for the sake of curiosity, but people are naturally interested in other people, and the memories of our tourist guests are more apt to be enriched by contact with people of a different culture than from a tour of ancient ruins. Walking along the bank of the Tula River and browsing through the fields of Chapultepec and La Vina with our Otomi brothers in Christ, admiring and inquiring about the growing crops, always makes a delightful occasion for me, a pleasure undiminished by the passage of years. For fifteen years we have made at least one trip annually into Mexico, and for probably five of these years I have made two trips.

On one of our visits to Colony Hill, we found something new sitting in Venancio's courtyard beside the corncrib and tractor. It was a fully-equipped, four-wheel-drive jeep — a gift from a California man who had visited Otomi country, observing there

On Colony Hill brow a young wife holds a goat kid in her arms. She is standing in an enclosure formed by shrubs cut and tightly fitted. The shurbs are covered with needle-sharp thorns more than an inch long. Animals are placed in corrals like this at night to keep them safe from coyotes.

the church and activities of the believers. He had learned of Venancio's strenuous trips into the mountainous hinterland in the interest of the expanding church. A wonderful gift, we thought, and rejoiced that it came at such an opportune time. These continuous trips north, with poor transportation, poor connections, and hiking rough trails, were exhausting Venancio's strength so that his usual excellent health was being affected. At first, Venancio used the services of one of the believers as chauffeur. He learned to drive in a year or two, however, and then could come and go as he needed. He could take someone with him if necessary and rest when he wished, thus accomplishing more while conserving his time and strength. This jeep was a God-sent gift, therefore, and the man who gave it was another example of what it's all about. God brings about the strangest combinations of circumstances to get the right people to the appointed place at the exact time to accomplish His purposes. That is the reason we have taken people to see the mission field on every opportunity that offered.

With such a rich storehouse of friendships, experiences, observations, and conclusions, how could we refrain from sharing with Christian friends and business people our adventures on the mission fields, when possible, by taking them on tours, or here at home by telling the story by word or colored slides? Why

The author and wife have a pair of two year old Otomi namesakes. They are cousins, children of sisters. Armando on the right and Elvira on the left.

wouldn't we acquaint our friends with the powerful Wycliffe drama, as it is being enacted around the world? Why wouldn't we hold in highest esteem these great missionaries who have taught us so much? By the same token, I couldn't refuse the invitation to the Wycliffe Board to become their representative. Isn't it natural to want to share with others what one believes in? Everyone believes in something, and those who trust God's Word have the high privilege of knowing the truth which sets men free, the Bible being the ultimate basis of authority.

In addition to conducting dinner rallies, filling speaking engagements, and taking groups to see the mission field, I have frequently been invited to set up Wycliffe displays at Christian colleges, church missionary conferences, etc. Such displays consist of Wycliffe publications, enlarged pictures showing various phases of Wycliffe work, translated Scripture portions from languages and countries around the world, Wycliffe literacy materials which prepare illiterate people to read translated Scripture, and the ever-popular artifacts.

But top priority in presenting these displays was the opportunity to interest dedicated young Christians as new recruits, to inform and direct them toward the ministry of Bible translation as a life service. When I became a Wycliffe representative, I set a goal of enlisting a score or more of new recruits to go to mission fields — attained in 1970, just ten years after I had set it.

In the winter of 1965, my wife and I were made honorary members of the Mexico Branch of Wycliffe Bible Translators. This very nearly overwhelmed us, because in November, 1963, the Colombia Branch of Wycliffe had bestowed on us an identical honor. We deeply appreciated these acts of love and esteem, although we felt unworthy and undeserving. However, with the respect, sincerity, and affection we feel, we continue to tell the Wycliffe story wherever we go, and expect to as long as we live. We are forever grateful to Bob Collett for bringing Wycliffe Bible Translators and its work into our lives. I often wonder what our lives would be like today if we had allowed his exciting account of the Otomi of the Mezquital just to go in one ear and out the other. One thing we do know — we are far happier now than we were then. Therefore I represent and serve that in which I believe.

CHAPTER TWENTY
MISSIONARIES ARE PECULIAR

Where in the world do all the missionaries come from? I don't know where they all come from, but I do know where many of the more than 4,000 Wycliffe missionaries come from. The place is named in the question — from just about all over the world.

One of the loveliest Wycliffe members we know is a Mexican girl, Artemisa Echegoyen, serving as a missionary in her own country, among the Eastern Otomi people. She and her teammate, Katy Voightlander; translator and artist, have completed their New Testament translation and are now doing literacy work in their tribe.

Scores of other Wycliffe members have come from a variety of countries: Australia, Canada, Germany, Great Britain, New Zealand, Switzerland, and others, as well as hundreds from the United States. In addition, Wycliffe has received members from Belgium, Colombia, Denmark, Finland, France, Guyana, Hong Kong, Jamaica, Japan, Netherlands, Norway, Panama, Peru, the Republic of South Africa, Ghana, and Sweden.

Before I knew better, I thought all missionaries came from the United States and went to work mainly in India, Africa, and China. After we met and became acquainted with Wycliffe Bible Translators in Mexico in 1959, I learned that this was not true. Also I learned that missionaries are a peculiar people.

God told the children of Israel, His chosen people, that they should be a "peculiar" people — that if they would believe on Him, trust Him, call upon Him, obey Him, and love Him with all their hearts, they would be peculiar to the rest of the world. In our day, rarely does anyone want to be considered peculiar. However, if one believes in the Lord Jesus Christ, trusts Him, calls upon Him, obeys Him, and loves Him with all his heart, he cannot escape being considered peculiar, in the eyes of this present muddled world. Missionaries, therefore, to be God's choice, will be considered peculiar — and so they are, in a very precious, special way. They are different from the run-of-the-mill folks you pass on the sidewalk, compete with in businss or athletics, and from whom you buy your clothes.

They have met Christ, and that life-changing experience has caused a transformation in thought, word, and deed. Through His influence, they have rearranged priorities to put others before themselves. Many have relinquished opportunities for outstanding success in their chosen field, with the accompanying recognition and financial reward. Others have passed up teaching positions in prestigious universities, or a chance to marry the banker's daughter — all in order to live in a foreign culture among unlovely people who have never heard that there is only one true and living God whose mercy is everlasting, who have never heard the message of love from His Word. Why, the world asks, would thousands and thousands of intelligent and educated people choose to do a thing like that?

Deciding to go to the mission field isn't an experience like being struck by lightning. It is more like the decision to plant a field. It takes time, thought, and patient waiting for the right season — God's time. Some people's minds were turned toward the mission field early in life — in childhood. Others answered a call while they were in college or nurses' training. Still others put off deciding until they were engaged in business or occupying a pulpit. Each has a story of his own, all as different as thumb prints or the infinite variety of snowflakes. After listening to the stories of two or three hundred Wycliffe recruits as they passed through the Mexico Branch headquarters en route to Chiapas for survival training at Jungle Camp, I was astounded at the way God works to bring about the right circumstances at the right time to fill His ranks with the right people.

At the time I became Wycliffe representative in Indianapolis and in Indiana, I had already made up my mind that mission field recruits were top priority, so I decided to set a goal of finding twenty or more. I had no idea how long it would take or how it would be done. But by this time I felt that the best place for a church to find some missionaries to send out was among their own young people, so the best place to start telling the Wycliffe story would be in my own church. I did this, and had not one but two first recruits from my church, and the church sent them out with full support. They each have an interesting story, so perhaps I shall tell them, along with half a dozen others, hoping they will stimulate the interest of recruits and recruiters. Wycliffe alone needs 2500 more translators and literacy specialists to complete the task in this generation.

My first two recruits, Francine Derk and Doris Lee Schuler, came so close together that I called them both winners. Both came out of my home church and soon became our pride and joy. When they arrived in Mexico for the Jungle Camp phase of their training, they immediately became known as "the Dawson girls." Francine called us Aunt Vera and Unk. Lee called us Pop and Mom.

Soon after I was appointed Wycliffe representative, we began inviting Wycliffeites to be our house guests while in Indianapolis. Several accepted, and their names began to fill the pages of our missionary guest book. Whenever they stayed overnight, we began inviting the young people of our church in for the evening to get acquainted and hear reports from the fields. The kids liked to come, so often we had a dozen or two in for pictures, missionary experiences, fun, and snacks.

Autumn came and with it the annual scheduled missionary conference in our church. That year the principal conference speakers were Norman Lewis of Back to the Bible, and Ethel Wallis of Wycliffe Bible Translators. These two excellent speakers complemented each other, making a challenging team. Services were held at 10:00 a.m. each day and at 7:00 in the evening. The team especially emphasized the blessings in store for the church which sent its own, and by the middle of the week young people were becoming serious.

In June of that year Francine Derk had graduated from college, a denominational school noted for its emphasis on missions and its strong preparatory courses for young people called to the mission field. As soon as she was graduated, Francine applied to that church's mission board for permission to go to their mission field, but was rejected on the grounds that she had not specialized. She was therefore not qualified to teach, preach, but only to be used in administration if needed. She returned home a brokenhearted girl, embarrased, hurt, and in despair. As soon as she recovered from the initial shock and disappointment, she accepted a job teaching weekday religious education in one of the Indianapolis schools. She was faithful in attendance at church, singing in the choir and teaching children. Although she somewhat regained her cheery disposition, she failed to regain her soaring spirit which had been almost destroyed by being deprived of an opportunity to fulfill her childhood dream.

As she attended the current missionary conference every day, her desire to go to the mission field almost overwhelmed her, only to be batted down like a tennis ball by the fact that she had been rejected in June.

During conference week, Ethel Wallis was our houseguest. One day in the middle of the week, we were on our way home for lunch, following the 10:00 a.m. service. Francine was with us, as we had invited her to have lunch with us, and I turned to her and asked, "Francine, why don't you go to the Summer Institute of Linguistics next summer, in preparation to go to a Wycliffe field?" "Because I'm not smart enough," she answered right back. "I was turned down by a board which didn't require linguistics. I could never learn to be a linguist."

"Sure you could, Francine," Ethel quickly assured her. "You are the kind that make the best translators. You **are** smart — and you'll be surprised how God helps those who have a strong desire to be linguistic missionaries." For a moment or two Francine was quiet, and then she brought out, "Besides that, it takes money to go to SIL — and I don't have any."

"I know someone who would love to send you to two terms of SIL, and it wouldn't cost you one dime," I told her.

That stopped the conversation. The next day, after the 10:00 a.m. conference session, Francine came up to me and said, "Did you really mean it when you said that you knew someone who would send me to SIL?"

I looked her straight in the eyes and assured her, "I sure did mean it. I know someone and know him well. He will be the happiest guy in town to send you to SIL."

"You know, I've just about decided to accept the chance to go — if you and Ethel think I'm smart enough," she said thoughtfully. "Will you be my Unk?"

"Gladly, Francine," I replied. "I will be your Unk for keeps."

By the end of the conference week, Doris Lee Schuler, the daughter of a Presbyterian pastor in Florida who was employed as a Registered Nurse in Indianapolis, became very much interested in the mission field. She was a member of our church, but she was hearing about pioneer missions for the first time. She had read all the Wycliffe brochures and was asking all sorts of intelligent questions. Lee and Francine were friends and had no doubt been talking together all week. It was not surprising, therefore, that when Norman Lewis made his challenge at the end of the last conference service and "drew the net" for young people interested in going to the mission field, Francine and Lee responded. Francine announced her intention of going to SIL for Wycliffe, and Lee reported that she was going also — they planned to go as a team. At once we had a pair — my first two recruits.

Francine and Lee roomed together during two terms of SIL at Norman, Oklahoma, and as soon as the last session ended, they made application for membership with Wycliffe Bible Translators. Needless to say, they were enthusiastically accepted. Probably within 15 minutes thereafter we learned about it through a phone call, as did everyone else within reasonable hearing distance in Norman, Oklahoma.

The two girls went to Mexico together for Jungle Camp training. At Main Base they were roommates and at Advance Base they built their **champa** (shelter made of available materials) together and shared it. The Jungle Camp staff noted the unusual energy they demonstrated, for when other trainees were worn down almost to a crawl, the "Dawson girls" were just gaining momentum. They became known as the happiest and most fun-loving team in Mexico. Eventually they parted, however, when Francine felt the call to Papua New Guinea and Lee chose to go to the Philippines.

Since most of Francine's support was assured, her deputation period was relatively short, and soon she was on her way to Papua New Guinea where she was assigned to work among the Rawa people. Even though Lee's support was largely provided for, her period of deputation was somewhat extended. During her jungle training in Mexico, a fellow trainee from Washington, William Hall, took special notice of her, and on the way back to the States, he told her so, much to her surprise. Since they were both prepared to go to a Wycliffe mission field, that was a good starting place to find out what else they had in common. Bill, also, was assigned to the Philippines, and he soon realized that the special attraction he had felt at Jungle Camp was not in vain. They soon knew they were in love, and Bill asked Lee to marry him. Bill still lacked a portion of his support, but with her family in Florida and his in Seattle, the prospects seemed bright.

On the afternoon of President Kennedy's assassination in Dallas, Bill and Lee were married by her father in his church in Ormand Beach, Florida. A charming couple, gifted in platform speaking, their successful deputation soon made it possible for them to be on their way to the Philippines. There they were assigned to work among the Subanon people, located on the southwest tip of Mindanao in a village called Siocon.

A Canadian girl was Francine's first partner among the Rawas. They had their house built in the village and were well into the language, able to communicate and adapting well to the culture when, as sometimes happens, the Canadian partner fell in love with an Australian lad and they were married. This of course took her away from Francine and the Rawa work, and also necessitated Francine's move out of the tribal village, since single girls can only serve in a tribe as a team.

It would take more than this to upset the versatile Francine, however. She moved back to Ukarumpa, the Wycliffe center in the highlands, where she continued to work on her language, served in the commissary, and as hostess in the guest house, and at other times operated the base radio which connected all tribe personnel with the center. She also worked in the print shop and publications department, and at anything else that needed to be done, coping with whatever need arose.

While she was thus occupied, a tall, blonde, brilliant boy

from a Kansas farm who was also a translator, began taking special notice of this vivacious single girl without a partner. And again it happened, as it frequently seems to, the shy, quiet, serious young man married the breezy, fun-loving, capable girl — a good combination on the farm or the mission field. Oren Claassen was a nephew of Theodore Epp, Founder and Director of Back to the Bible Broadcast in Lincoln, Nebraska, and this team set up one of the happiest homes in Papua New Guinea. Now we had become "Aunt Vera and Unk" to the Claassens and "Pop and Mom" to the Halls. Our hearts were divided between Papua New Guinea and the Philippines, and we vowed to ourselves, "We must visit them."

The right time came in 1967, and we spent two weeks with each of the girls and their husbands — with the Halls in the Philippines and the Claassens in Papua New Guinea. These girls were as our own daughters, so the visits were sheer delight to them and to us. Company from home is a great occasion for missionaries of the field, and is also a great source of encouragement to them.

By this time Lee and Bill had two youngsters whom we had not yet seen. The noon of the day following our arrival in Manila, we received a wire from Bill and Lee, telling us that Tammy, their two-year-old daughter, had meningitis and was in the hospital at Zamboanga City, on the tip of the southwest peninsula of Mindanao.

We flew there on the first plane possible and remained until Tammy was able to leave the hospital, with good chances for recovery. Wanting me to visit their allocation among the Subanon, Bill arranged for he and I to fly to Siocon and back that evening. We took along a cargo of aluminum corregated roofing to cover a portion of their house so they could collect rainwater. The remainder of the roof was of palm thatch. Since their house was miles from the little airport at Siocon, Bill asked for the privilege of our hanging onto the frame of a logging truck which was going to a sawmill fairly close to their home. I shall never know how we hung onto the running gears of that logging truck, as it raced and bounced over a rough dirt road, going around corners at the same speed, never looking back to see if we were still hanging on or caring whether or not we had dropped by the wayside. Since it was too great a distance to walk it, we had three choices — not to go, to hang on, or to fall off. Thirty minutes later, when they stopped, I was the happiest man in the Philippines.

We ate our lunch which we had carried from Zamboanga City, in Lee and Bill's house which sat high on stilts and was reached by climbing a ladderlike stairs. Then we took a long walk to visit with the Subanon. Before the afternoon was over, we had waded a shallow stream a dozen times or more. Bil and Lee experience all the problems of a mission field in Mexico or Latin America, and a couple of trials they do not have. The Siocon Subanon do not live in villages like the Indians of South America, but are scattered to the four winds. They do not come to the missionary; instead the missionary has to travel long distances to be a part of this people. It takes a lot of precious time and is expensive.

Scattered up and down the west coast of the peninsula from Zamboanga City to well beyond Subanon territory are villages and cove pockets of Moslems. They are largely pirates and smugglers, but are fanatically devoted to their Moslem belief. Their occupation of piracy and smuggling requires them to be belligerent and brutal. They do influence the atmosphere and the natural disposition of the Subanon environment.

The Halls do have one problem that is common to Latin America missionaries. Sorcery, witchcraft, and superstition run hand in hand with spiritualism, ancestor worship, feeding of the dead, and fear of the night. That afternoon, as we were crossing and recrossing the ankle-deep stream, meeting the people, visiting little homes, and watching farmers working with water buffalo, we came to a larger house on the creek bank, built on a steep rise. Bill told us that it was the home of a sorceress. She had become acquainted with Lee and Bill and was interested in what they were doing among the Subanon, but being friendly did not affect her practice of sorcery.

Bill thought she might feel complimented if he took North American guests to meet her, so we turned in and climbed the hill, then the steep steps to her house on stilts. She graciously received us and acknowledged the introduction. She did not arise as we were ushered into her room by her sister who lived with her and acted as an assistant. She was sitting in the middle of the floor with her long circular skirt spread all around her, far beyond her feet.

Before we reached the house, Bill had told us about her. He said it was claimed that she was qualified to be a sorceress because she had seven toes on her feet. During our visit, Paul Carlson, the JAARS pilot who flew us to Siocon in a Helio Courier plane and remained with us in order to fly us back to Zamboanga that evening, was making this series of visits with us and was sitting on the floor like the rest of us. He wanted to change his position a litle, so he stood up and took a step backward. Being a camera fan, he had a couple of them dangling from his neck. When he stood, he took hold of one camera to stop its swinging.

This created quite a commotion, because to the sorceress it appeared that he was going to take her picture. Since being photographed is one of the worst things that could happen to her, she became so perturbed that she accidentally got one foot out from under the hem of her very long dress. Sure enough! She was qualified to be a sorceress because she had seven toes on at least one foot. It took all the rest of our visit for Bill to explain, apologize, get Paul seated again, and then graciously get us all excused so we could fly back to the city before dark. I have never decided who profited from that visit — certainly not the sorceress.

Tammy did completely recover without bad aftereffects. Bill and Lee did find a language helper and a fellowship with the scattered people, learned their language, and with the help of linguistic workshops, made good progress in translation. Bill became helpful to other linguists in the process of time, and his Branch recommended that he come to the States for his Ph.D. studies in Advanced Linguistics, in preparation to serve as a consultant in their Linguistic Workshops. (The services of workshops and consultants considerably shorten the time required to translate a New Testament.) We knew that Bill and Lee and their family still considered us as "Pop" and "Mom" when they drove hundreds of miles to attend our golden wedding reception in June, 1975.

Douglas Hunt, the New Zealand JAARS pilot, flew us from Lae to the Ukarumpa Center, in Papua New Guinea, using the two-motor Piper Aztec plane. Just as soon as possible, we were delivered to the door of the prettiest cottage on the street. The walkways and borders were lined with blooming flowers, and the yard was as clean as a pin. It was the kind of place we had imagined theirs would be. The front door burst open and out Francine bounced, laughing and crying with joy, dragging Oren to meet his new Aunt and "Unk"-in-law. What a reunion! It was worth the trip just to see this first outburst of delight and genuine happiness. Her spirit soared again because she was exactly where she wanted to be. At last she had attained her childhood dream. The former Francine was living again.

Oren was a prince, with all the traits of a pedigreed missionary. He was pleasant, thoughtful, poised, brilliant, refined, and gifted in the art of making, fixing, and creating things with his hands, which is so essential on the mission field. He was the kind of a son that would make any dad and mother proud. Here was a team that complemented each other in every way, and Papua New Guinea was fortunate to have them.

Francine had worked more than a year in the Rawa village

where she and her former partner had been allocated. She was well acculturated to the new life, had made friends readily, and was soon able to conquer enough language to communicate regarding basic things. However, now that Oren was to become her husband-partner in the same Rawa village, a problem arose that had to be resolved. It just wasn't advisable for a couple to go to any tribal village when the wife knew the language and the husband didn't. A husband must be as smart as his wife, to be respected. The solution was for both to remain in Ukarumpa, and bring a bright villager to the Center for the purpose of teaching the husband Rawa so that he would become as smart as his wife.

Immediately they sent for two young men to come to Ukarumpa — one a good language teacher and one to help with chores around the premises. These young fellows came to the Center where one poured Rawa language into Oren's ears morning, noon, and night. In our town we would call it a "crash course." Francine kept happy and busy, keeping house, keeping store, operating radio communications, working in publications, and planning a new house to be built at the Center as soon as it was advisable, after spending a year in the village.

We had great visits with Ron and Ruth Gluck, who had a guest room for us, flew to Kelobo to visit Dennis and Nancy Cochrane who worked among the Dunas, drove with Darlene Bee and Vida Chenoweth to their Usarufa village for three days, and were entertained for evening meals all over Ukarumpa.

All too soon our two weeks were nearly over. Then came the bitter process of bidding all of these wonderful friends goodbye and wishing them God's blessings. It was extremely hard to break away from all our loved ones, but we left with a rewarding consolation — that we had kept our promise to visit both our girls on their fields.

In record time, Oren absorbed Rawa like a sponge and soon became as smart as his wife, much to the delight of his language helper. He took great pride in Oren and was anxious to take them back to his village where he would be greatly respected.

In due time they moved back to the Rawa village, repaired their house, learned more and more language, and laid out a new airstrip. The villagers became interested and volunteered to work with both Oren and Francine in manually constructing a village airstrip so that JAARS planes could safely land and take off with load limits. It took backbreaking work for months, but it saved hours of travel and hardships in commuting back and forth from the village to the Center.

Days, weeks, and months passed quickly, with Oren and

Francine making the most of the time. Language study forged ahead. Oren began compiling material in recorded form for translation, literacy, grammar, literature, and a dictionary, while Francine continually had congregations of children and adults eager to be taught. Her fabulous gift for storytelling began to make little Rawa eyes pop wide in expectation, just like little Indianapolis eyes.

While we were at Ukarumpa, Oren and Francine had selected a lot next to their best friends, on which to build a new base house, as soon as it was advisable. They proudly had set out two trees in anticipation. The right time did come, and they built and tastefully furnished a new house and enjoyed a little while in it before they came back to the States on their furlough.

Not many months after their return to their home and work in Papua New Guinea, Mrs. Homiak, Francine's mother, received the extremely joyous news that her daughter was expecting a baby. Mail service hustled happy letters back and forth between Indianapolis and Ukarumpa, interspersed with little packages to Papua New Guinea, as the months slowly passed. Then came the heartbreaking news that the lovely son born to Oren and Francine had only lived a few hours. No couple was ever more disappointed or grieved, because they had great plans for their lives with a child. On the other hand, no couple other than a missionary couple could more sincerely say, "It was God's will to take him, and God never makes a mistake." Because of their great faith, this was exactly what they said and meant.

With the passing of time, Francine regained her strength and together by faith they rose above their disappointment, grief and heartache and plunged into their work with a renewed determination. Francine added activities as her strength permitted, while Oren continued with his language work in and out of their Rawa village, adding stacks of pages of analysis to his complicated and priceless manuscript.

* * * * * * * * *

Long before it was daylight, on the morning of April 7, 1972, our telephone in Bradenton, Florida, rang loudly to awaken us from sound sleep. Ben Elson's voice came across the wire from Santa Ana, California, saying "Just five hours ago, the Piper Aztec in Papua New Guinea was involved in a serious accident and several of our people were aboard." I couldn't wait any longer, and asked, "Were Oren and Francine hurt?"

"Oren and Francine were killed," he answered. "The plane exploded just before it landed, and all seven people were killed."

"Was there anyone else that we knew?" I asked.

115

He named them all. In addition to Oren and Francine, there were two more of our very close friends — Douglas Hunt, the pilot, and Dr. Darlene Bee. The other three we did not know. Two were translation helpers and the other a Wycliffe girl who had been working in Lae.

We were stunned and speechless. What can one appropriately say in response to such tragic news? We found and gave Dr. Elson the telephone number of Francine's parents, and told him what time it would be in Indianapolis. What does one say about a sudden crushing event like this, even after he has time to think? Can one say anything better than Francine and Oren said when they lost their child — "It had to be God's will, and God never makes mistakes."

An impressive and sacred funeral service was held in Papua New Guinea, with seven coffins lined up side by side. Francine and Oren were buried beside their infant son. We flew at once to Indianapolis to comfort Francine's parents, and so that I might participate in the memorial service on Sunday afternoon, with relatives from Pennsylvania and hundreds of friends of Francine Derk Claassen attending.

This sunny, talented missionary girl had packed more living into those short years than many who had lived their three score and ten. It will never be known how many lives were made better in the United States, Mexico, and Papua New Guinea by the words, faith, and influence of my first missionary recruit.

The ones to whom Oren's manuscript was especially valuable were Don and Norma Toland, the couple who took the place of Oren and Francine among the Rawa. One might think that such a tragic event which took seven lives would tend to slow down the flow of missionary recruits. Instead, it had the opposite effect and if anything, it increased the flow of recruits. Very few Wycliffe stories have tragic endings, for which credit is primarily due to the jungle survival training, a phase of the Wycliffe training program, which prepares each candidate for the rigors of primitive living in rugged environments.

Recruiting for missions is a continual challenge to me, and I'm always looking forward to my next such adventure and its outcome. In July, 1964, in Bogota, Colombia, South America, I met a personable young fellow, Keith Forster of Johannesburg, Republic of South Africa. He had come from Bible college to spend three months of his summer vacation setting up a workable bookkeeping system for Wycliffe's Bogota offices. In South Africa he had prepared himself to become a Certified Public Accountant and had entered this profession. A Christian with a warm heart toward missions, by a strange coincidence he had seen a film on the work of Wycliffe Bible Translators. Later he found a book describing their activities among people who had no written language. Astonished that there were so many tongues spoken and so few written, and realizing that those unwritten languages had no Bible, he began to reconsider the career he was pursuing. After months of investigation and fulfilling both African and United States requirements, he gained entry into the States and then into Columbia Bible College in Columbia, South Carolina, where he began preparation for some mission field. I had a few days to become acquainted with him and grew to like him very much. As soon as school convened in the fall, Keith went back to Columbia Bible College for his senior year.

During the spring of 1965, I was passing through Columbia, and as it was near noon, I decided to go out to the college and take two or three of our Indianapolis young people out to lunch. When we arrived, I could not find even one of the Indianapolis kids anywhere. I didn't see anyone I knew except Keith Forster who was in the dining room, but had eaten his lunch.

Keith seemed reserved and a bit discouraged, so I decided to take a little walk with him and visit. He said school was going quite well, and he was assured of graduation in June. Of course I asked, "Then what? Are you going to the mission field?" He described his predicament to me. He was in this country on a student visa, and he was not allowed to work for wages. And even though he felt the call to a mission field, he could not finance further preparation or solicit support. Besides, there was a special Canadian girl in Columbia Bible College who did not feel any inclination to go to the mission field. He felt it would take a lot of praying and deep thinking to solve all of these complications. He hated to give up the lovely girl for the mission field, and if he chose the mission field it seemed hopelessly far away.

Then I gave him a real problem. I said, "Keith, while you're waiting for developments, why don't you plan to go to the Summer Institute of Linguistics as soon as school is out? Then if Wycliffe looks good to you, continue through the second term, go to Jungle Camp, and see what happens? My wife and I are looking for another 'Dawson boy,' and we will gladly send you — without any string attached."

He became very quiet and was slow to answer. Then he said, "What more could a person wish? It seems incredible for you, almost a stranger, to be so interested and generous with one like me. I cannot accept now, neither can I reject. However, I must and will find out exactly what the Lord wants me to do. I shall pray and grapple with this whole matter, and then make a decision as I know I will inevitably have to do. Will you allow me to write you as soon as I know?"

117

We thought he would write in a few days, but a month or more went by, and there was no word from Keith. I began to think I had offended him — but sure enough, one day his letter came. It was a very positive letter. His decision was to accept our offer to send him to SIL, and he would apply at once. He felt that he must go to the mission field, and this was God's way of getting him there. He and his girl friend, Wilma, had a prolonged discussion. She would be most happy to be his wife in Canada or any business location, but not on the mission field. Therefore, they decided to go their separate ways.

Probably a year and a half later, my wife and I were in Mexico, and we flew down to San Cristobal Las Casas, capital of the State of Chiapas and also the jumping-off place for Wycliffe recruits on their way to Jungle Camp. Some of the stores there were favorite places for Jungle Campers to do last-minute shopping. We were browsing through one of these places, and found many U.S. young people there because a new session of Jungle Campers were in town waiting for Missionary Aviation Fellowship (MAF) planes to fly them out next day.

A lovely young lady stepped up to us and called us by name. She said, "I know who you are, although I haven't met you before. I'm Wilma, Keith Forster's fiancee, and I'm on my way in to Jungle Base. When that training is finished, Keith and I are to be married, and we are then assigned to Colombia, South America." We were delighted but not too surprised to learn that the young lady had changed her mind. Just another answer to prayer. When Panama was annexed to Colombia as a mission field of Wycliffe, Keith and Wilma were transferred to Panama. They have two children and work among the Paya Cuna.

Something very similar happened to our "yard boy" in Indianapolis. When Ron Stoltzfus got big enough to ride the tractor at the farm, he sent his little brother to mow our yard. Ron chose to go to Colombia Bible College when he graduated from high school, and he too fell in love with an undergraduate, a petite girl who was the daughter of missionaries to the West Indies. Ron, his parents and family, belonged to our missionary church, so he was mission-field oriented from every direction. He knew the Wycliffe story and liked it, so one day while he was a college Junior, I asked him, "Ron, as soon as you are graduated, why don't you go to the Summer Institute of Linguistics and see what happens?" He pretty much knew what would happen, so he said, "I wouldn't mind going, but I don't think I want to go so soon." I knew why he was dragging his feet, so I waited a year and asked him the same question. By that time he was a little more frank and open. He said, "You know, there is this sweet little girl Sharon that I think the world of. I think maybe she might want to go to the mission field also, after she has graduated a couple of years from now, and it might be nice to go to SIL together."

But he did confer with SIL administrators, and they advised him to take at least one term of SIL upon graduation, for a very special reason. He took their advice and did very well that first year, showing excellent talent for an assignment in Mexico. The Wycliffe Candidate Secretary was also very interested in Sharon, but they urged Ron to take his second term at once, and to be assigned to Mexico. A replacement was urgently needed for Dr. John Crawford, head of the Linguistic Survey Department of the Mexico Branch, and Ron was being groomed for this — an important assignment because its work was to determine how many more tribes needed translators, and how many more linguistic teams would be needed to finish the work in Mexico. Such an assignment for Ron would not in any way hinder Sharon's progress, and the Mexico Branch would benefit while Sharon caught up with Ron. Ron did a great job which won praise from Dr. Joe Grimes, a linguistic specialist. Sharon finished her college, taught school a term, and worked in two terms of SIL, even before Ron finished the survey. They were married, and she was assigned to Mexico.

All the time until furlough year they kept their eyes open for a difficult tribal area which appeared to need them most, as a place to settle when they came back. Ron was urged to study Advanced Linguistics at Cornell during furlough year. He did this and they accomplished the required deputation despite some sickness and surgery, and returned to Mexico determined to get into one of the most difficult areas geographically that one could imagine. They asked to be allocated among the Guarojio Indians and went about getting settled in and a warm house built before cold weather. Ron and Sharon have the special mettle which gives them the devotion, zeal, inward strength, wisdom, perseverance, unselfishness, and faith required to take their little family into hard-to-reach places, in Jesus' name. I know, because I watched Ron grow up. They will get their New Testament finished in record time.

I believe it was in the spring of 1968 that I planned to fly to Mexico City to attend a conference for a week. Three young ladies who attended our church had become interested in Wycliffe, and all of them wished to go to Mexico to see a bit of the mission field. I suggested it would be nice for them to see something of Wycliffe's Mexico fields while I attended conference. They liked the idea and made arrangements to be away from their duties. One taught first grade in a Christian school, while the other two were Registered Nurses. I wrote to a friend of ours, a Mexican translator, Artemisa Echegoyen, asking if she would room with the girls and act as their hostess, interpreter, and guide, showing them as much as possible in a week. It turned out to be the greatest week possible for the three Indianapolis guests. Artemisa took the girls by bus, horseback, Mexican bush plane (held together with baling wire and twine string), and by foot to visit her Eastern Otomi village for a couple of days and nights. They appeared to be well indoctrinated, because as they took turns sitting beside me in the plane flying 2500 miles back to Indianapolis, each related a continuous list of experiences with the lovely villagers in Artemisa's Otomi tribe. As a result, two of the girls made application to attend SIL in Norman that summer, but before the third could make her arrangements, she was stricken with a serious illness. Rosemary Gingery, the schoolteacher, took her two terms of SIL with literacy in mind, and after Jungle Camp training, was assigned to Bolivia to work in literacy among the Guarani people. She and her partner are doing a great job, and there appears to be a possibility that the girls may cross into Argentina, since the Guarani people live on both sides of the border. Sharon Hinschman, the nurse who took SIL training, chose later to go to work in Brazil with the Unevangelized Fields Mission. Nellie Collins, the other nurse, had cancer which was successfully arrested. She felt that she was not able to work on a foreign field, however, she continued her nursing at home and is actively engaged during her free time in a home mission project among discouraged cancer patients everywhere. Thus Artemisa shares credit with me in gaining a missionary for Wycliffe, as well as one for another foreign service, and one at home. We won't quibble about where they serve, as long as they bring glory to the Lord.

There appears to be no set way to find recruits. I think of missions as contagious, something like the measles. If enough people are exposed, a good percent of them will "take it." Several that I have not described or named filled their slots in the Lord's service, as well. Some came from the farm, one was an assistant to a pastor, one married a second-generation Wycliffe girl. One read a book, another saw a film, still another heard a speaker. Another asked for an interview, one shared a trip to Waxhaw for an interview. But last, yet most important, they were all prayed for.

This crop of missionary recruits gave me the pride and feeling of satisfaction that I used to experience when harvest was over for the year, while I was a farmer. Mows full of hay and at the elevator, barns of cattle and pens of calves, sows and pigs — were what I had to show for a hard year's work.

A harvest of missionaries, busy all over the world, is something pretty special to be proud of. You know what? I have hobnobbed so much with missionaries that I'm peculiar too.

CHAPTER TWENTY-ONE
WHAT MAKES THE OTOMI TICK?

If one attempts to analyze and explain the nobility, the grandeur, of Otomi character — the integrity, the perseverance, the faithfulness, the spiritual ascendancy of these people — he will eventually conclude that the key to this success story lies in the life of Venancio Hernandez, the over-shepherd of the Otomi flock.

Venancio was born to poor Otomi parents living at or near San Nicolas, the first village east of Ixmiquilpan. In order to survive in this arid land, every member of the family had to work. If the parents could not afford to own animals, the logical task for a child was to herd goats and sheep for a neighbor. As soon as he was old enough, therefore, Venancio assumed such a responsibility.

His parents could neither read nor write and spoke only Otomi, but Venancio was a bright child, possessing an avid thirst for learning. Early in his life, a benevolent Mexican lady in San Nicolas took notice of the boy and one day asked him if he would like to speak, read, and write in Spanish. This was the highest dream of his young heart, so Venancio enthusiastically welcomed her offer. For a few hours each evening thereafter, he studied intensively and persevered until he could read. He practiced on everything written in Spanish that he could lay hands on. Thus he became literate in the language of his country, to be followed later by the study of literacy in the language of his people. It was unheard of for an Otomi boy to become bilingual so early in life, but since God had destined this boy to become the spiritual leader of his people, this was the logical first step in his preparation.

Several years later, Venancio was thumbing through the limited amount of literature available in the Ixmiquilpan market, nearly all of it in Spanish. As he leafed through the various volumes, he came upon a well-worn book with what seemed to

121

him an odd title, so he read a sentence here and there. Some of the excerpts he noted bordered on heresy, in the light of his parents' teachings. But even if it was difficult to understand, it was more challenging than the newspapers he had been reading. The realization that it might be a controversial book and one that could not safely be read in the company of others, only increased his desire to learn of its contents. The price was one peso, and since he had that many centavos, he bought the Spanish New Testament, quickly tucked it under his coat, and disappeared in the market crowd. In his heart, he knew that such a book would be forbidden by his parents and condemned by everyone of his acquaintance. He must keep it a secret, only opening and reading it when he was alone in the desert with the goats and sheep.

The secret things that he read, as he eagerly turned the pages of the Book, were mysterious and confusing, but they were so fascinating that he could not discard it. For months he continued to read the pages of the Spanish New Testament, trying to discover what so magnetized him in this Book, when it was so hated by his people. It seemed innocent enough, but it was surely too complex for his understanding. He daily wrestled with its mysteries that he could not solve, no matter how many times he went over them. He believed as much as he comprehended, but he realized that he must find a hidden key, before he could enter into its wisdom with understanding.

One day he followed one of the commands contained in the Book, and he prayed. It was the essential prayer of repentance and acknowledgment of Jesus Christ as being the Son of God — the prayer of acceptance and faith required to become a true believer. Since, with this confession and acceptance, Venancio had fulfilled the requirements as given in the Book in order to receive a revelation from the Lord, so alone and unaided by man, he became a "new creature" in Christ Jesus, and old things passed away, all things became new (II Cor. 5:17). Now he understood what he had been reading for such a long time, and he began to trust and believe, unto unquestioning obedience.

These were experiences he could not keep to himself, for even his countenance betrayed him. But there were so very few that he dared to tell. Yet tell he must, and he decided the first should be Tito, his cousin. Tito was easily led to become a believer — then there were two, then three and more, being taught, praying, and growing into a strong, devout nucleus. After much bitter rejection of her husband's new belief, and long procrastination, Venancio's young wife, with fear and trembling, came to believe. Soon there were a dozen, then a score, who followed by faith into this strange new Way of Life.

As was to be expected, hatred and then persecution, both mental and physical, flared and spread in the same ratio that people broke away from the customs and traditions of their ancestors. Many suffered abuse, even from members of their own families and relatives. Many had to flee for their lives from hotheaded radicals. Others were not so fortunate as to escape. They, like Teofilo's nineteen-year-old son, paid for their newfound faith with their lives. To this day, many believers bear marks of persecution on their bodies.

One day as we rode along the road leading to El Olivo and Deca with the Sinclairs, we passed a place called El Spiritu. While we looked at it from the roadside, the Sinclairs described the public burial ground in connection with the village, the site of overwhelming heartbreak for dozens of believers. The infant death rate was always high among believers and unbelievers alike. When the infant of a believer's family died, the parents were denied the privilege of giving their child a Christian burial. A body had to be buried within twenty-four hours after death, so the parents were automatically thrown into impossible situations, just another part of the high price new converts had to pay to become followers of the Lord Jesus Christ.

Venancio was with us that day, and the Sinclairs asked him in Otomi for a word to describe the mental pain and anguish connected with finding a place to bury the body of a believer. He shook his head sadly, then spoke to Isabel at length, asking her to interpret to us.

"The believers have endured many dark days and nights of tribulation," he related. "It is a horrifying experience to try to deal fairly with drunken radicals. Almost every man was dismissed from his job when he became a convert. A friend of mine, Erasto, was stoned by a mob and left for dead. But the Lord revived him in the night, hours later, as his family prayed at home. He survived torturous persecution, amazed his enemies by his miraculous recovery, and still lives a victorious life."

Turning to the northwest, Venancio pointed and continued, "Do you see that first mountain range running toward Zimapan? When I was a young man, a friend and I fled three days and nights up into that mountainous country, pursued by a crowd of armed fanatics who believed the way to put a stop to this curse of evangelicalism was to destroy its leaders. God caused us to escape, because we were needed to nurture and care for the new believers. Had it not been for the peace in our hearts and minds, and the love we bore even towards our enemies, many would have turned back. Certainly no one enjoys persecution, but when we were sinners we were persecuted by fear, ignorance, and superstition. It was a far greater joy to be persecuted for the sake of Jesus Christ. Persecution came in waves. When many believers were being added to the church, the harassment intensified. On the other hand, when the cruelty increased, it invariably brought a new and large wave of believers."

Because of these problems, the believers petitioned the Mexican Government and were granted asylum to live on Colony Hill, near the Army Post. At the time of our first visit, approximately 150 Christians lived there, with more arriving steadily. This is a brief account of Venancio's faith and spiritual growth, a man greatly used of God to learn the Scriptures, trust the Word, obey God's commands, and impart the Good News to others.

Does Venancio have a title prefacing his name? Where did he receive his formal education and training?

His name is simply Venancio Hernandez. As to his education and training, it began with a Mexican neighbor lady of his childhood who taught him to read and write in Spanish. I am not certain when he became literate in Otomi. He received his knowledge of the Scriptures in the cactus desert where God revealed His plan of salvation and them impressed upon him that he should make disciples. But one can not call Venancio a self-made man; rather, he is a God-made man. I believe that in his private "upper room" God taught knowledge, wisdom, good judgment, and maturity to his servant, as he read, prayed, and meditated.

I am writing of one who possesses a personality that is altogether magnetic, captivating, and pervaded by God's Spirit. I have taken many Stateside pastors to the Mezquital to meet Venancio and his congregation. More than once I have heard the comments of these gentlemen who were spiritual leaders in their own parishes. I knew these men personally — among them my own pastor — and I have been in some of their churches. Their comments when they returned to Mexico City, or spoke again from their own pulpits, revealed the deep impressions made on their hearts. Of Venancio they said, "I felt that I should take off my shoes in his presence." . . . "In the company of that man, I felt as small as a schoolboy." . . . "Suddenly my own ministry became greatly minimized, as I observed him." . . . "I realized that he was a great man of God — no one had to tell me." . . .

Since in Christ "are hid all the treasures of wisdom and knowledge," (Col. 2:3) the Book that reveals Him is surely where Venancio finds his answers, gets his wisdom, his courage in leadership, and his spiritual poise. Those of us who do not have these attributes probably do not search the Scriptures thoroughly enough for God to honor our efforts, and especially our modern-day speed reading.

CHAPTER TWENTY-TWO
WHAT THE OTOMI TAUGHT US

In presenting this introduction to the culture, character, and life of the Otomi of the Mezquital, we have purposed to show, not what we could do for these people, but rather the indebtedness we feel for what they have done for us. The example of their dedicated lives, their suffering for Christ's name, their integrity, their simplicity of faith and action, have been a witness without parallel in our experience. Perhaps reading these observations will arouse and stimulate a desire for a deeper Christian dedication in your own life.

Primarily, we were shown that we had to quit playing church. It's a game that consumes nervous energy, wastes time, and produces no virtue. A good country club can do as much. Of what worth is it for a Christian to strive for goodness and respectability, and ignore or neglect the only real means of finding righteousness and peace for his soul through Jesus Christ, the one Way to God? The Otomi demonstrated this quite clearly to us.

Second, exemplified to us a humility we had never seen before. The Colony people were very poor when we first knew them, but ten years later they had become quite prosperous. Although they possessed land and God blessed the increase, no one built a new house, bought a new car, purchased a television set, or even a horse. I have never seen an Otomi wearing a matched suit of clothes. Yet they are clean, neat and tastefully groomed. They realized that soon they would need this new church, so as the Lord prospered them, they honored Him with the increase. And this church is certainly not a make-do structure, lacking facilities, merely a building with which to "get by." In fact, it has a baptistry of two full-sized sections. When we saw it in construction, I quipped to Venancio, "Are you going to have a 'his'n' and 'her'n' baptistries, a separate one for each?"

He threw back his head and laughed. "No," he explained, "when people gather here on special days like Christmas, Easter, New Year's, for conferences and rallies, many from small, distant churches wish to be baptized — sometimes eighty or a hundred people. If two of us are administering baptism at the same time,

What wisdom and common sense these people demonstrate. These are the things for which they saved their money and not for themselves.

Third, although this was not their intent, they taught us adventurous giving. We were led into this agricultural project without any preparation on our part. It really was not the normal thing for us to become so involved in someting so foreign to our way of life. But when we were confronted with the idea of putting the remaining half of our savings into an uncertain venture in a foreign country for the benefit of people we couldn't understand or converse with, it took a lot of heart searching, praying, and trust. To be compelled with an inward compulsion is a strange feeling, and there is no honest way to resist it. Since we knew this to be God's choice, we could only obey.

When I was a child, one Sunday morning I heard R. G. LeTourneau boom out in his emphatic voice, "You can't outgive God!" This Otomi farming adventure was a good way for us to prove it. We were sitting in ringside seats to observe what would happen. During the second and third years after we founded our agricultural project, fifty percent of our income was needed. Strangely enough, we saw our income increase in exact proportion to the rate of our giving. It seemed that God had His hands and eyes on this two-way street. Since our U.S. tax system honors deductions of 30%-50% given to charitable enterprises, we chose to take advantage of these benefits, because of our love for missions. A familiar standard prayer for us has become: "And Lord, parade before our eyes the places where you would choose for us to use your money." Little by little we began to enlarge the size of our list of competent and productive missionaries who needed additional support. In time it reached continuous partial support of twenty-four missionary families, serving over the world under five mission boards. Next thing we knew, we were formulating plans to include more in our personal missionary family, with provision to keep them on the mission field as long as their several tasks lasted, even after our deaths. A program like this will not increase your earthly treasures but it will bring down upon you an avalanche of love letters.

Fourth, we found that the secret of fast, steady growth in the Otomi church complex was that a believer naturally became an apostle. Lloyd Fesmire, pastor of Calvary Baptist Church of Bradenton, Florida, puts it this way: "Every Christian should be discipling someone." In our early days, we felt just like thousands of other nominal Christians. Our job was to get people into church so they could be exposed to the Gospel. Didn't we hire ministers for making believers? The Otomí changed our minds about that method.

Then this matter of carrying one's Bible to church. In some churches one is conspicuous when he does — in others, when he doesn't. We solved that problem in 1952. We carry our Bibles to church wherever we are, whether we are conspicuous or not. We have come to believe, like the Otomí, that one must bear a good testimony before saint and sinner alike. If the Bible is so important and precious to the Otomí believers that it goes to church wrapped in a plastic cover for protection, why should we do less?

The fifth, last, and perhaps the greatest lesson of all that Venancio and other Otomí Christians exemplify is their great ability to keep their horizon high. Venancio had his eyes on these congregations that were represented at the dedication of the new church, long before we knew this leader. In fact, a long time before he knew where these people existed — yes, even before he knew that there would be a place called Colony Hill.

I firmly believe that people make their own horizons. I don't know of anything more inconsistent and frustrating than for a layman, a pastor, or a church to have their horizon pulled down too low. Have you ever seen a cute little three-year-old step into his dad's empty boots and then pull daddy's hat down on his head? Everyone thinks it's fun to see the hat resting with the crown down over his ears, the brim supported by the bridge of his nose. All that he can see is his feet. When he starts to walk, he promptly falls down because he can't see where he's going. The solution is for someone to push the hat back so the brim rests on the back of his neck — which uncovers his eyes. What the person really did for him was to raise his horizon. However simple and naive it may sound to apply this to missions, haven't you many times heard the outworn phrase, "Missions start at home"? No one will dispute that. In fact, it's quite normal — but when in their hearts and under their breath they continue, "And end at home, too," — then it's a sure sign they haven't raised their horizon high enough. I know many of these, and most of them do not even support missions at home. They feel they just cannot afford it.

A number of our friends are pastors or laymen of denominational churches, and most of them support only missionaries of their own denomination. Often a list of their missionary families appears on a page of their church bulletin — frequently not over a dozen names. In some larger churches, where the name of the country may be listed after the name of the missionary, you may find that their entire list of missionaries serve in only one or two countries. And the congregation seems quite satisfied with this.

These locations are probably those of their first love — and they remain their only love. As a layman, I am aware of a clannish spirit among people (even those who love missions), among mission boards and even among missionaries. Wouldn't a greater blessing fall, if missionaries everywhere held hands, helping each other over obstacles of culture and language, striving to fan out, yet leaving no wide gaps in the over-all advance — that all may hear to the ends of the earth? To those who are willing to draw into their own little world and exclude everyone else, I keep asking the question, "What provision do you have to reach and take the Gospel to a quarter of a billion people who have never heard one verse of Scripture which names the Lord Jesus Christ, in isolated places like Nigeria, Brazil, India, Bangladesh, Indonesia, Papua New Guinea, the Philippines, Nepal, Australia? People tormented by evil spirits, fear, ignorance, and superstition just as Venancio said the Otomi were before they believed. Missions cannot stop on Main Street of the capitals of the nations — that is just where they start. The horizon is far beyond the cities. Most people get more excited over a broken fingernail or a piece of cold toast than they do over the fact that 4,138 languages have not a single word of Scripture, when there are already more than five hundred versions of the Bible in English. Since 1959 we have traveled around the world, looking into the "out-back" places of 24 nations. These experiences raised our horizon beyond our first love. By 1960 we were acquainted with a hundred missionaries, but now the number has increased to over five hundred, on many fields, working under several mission boards. And it was the Otomi of the Mezquital who started us out on these rewarding and pleasant journeys and experiences.

CHAPTER TWENTY-THREE
I PRESUME

I am certain that I have no right to judge, but I assume that one has a right to presume a few things. As I write of our happy experiences with the Otomi of the Mezquital and of Wycliffe Bible Translators, I hope it is possible that someone reading it may wish that they too had an interesting and rewarding project to explore and pursue. I presume that if my wife and I could experience a series of unplanned circumstances which led us to a happy ending, so others can do the same thing. We freely admit that ours came by Divine Providence. So can anyone else receive from the same Source, because we certainly have no monopoly on such blessings.

There is another way that I know whereby one may find worthwhile things to do. There are organized groups, chartered and incorporated, who are actually in the business of matchmaking, i.e., bringing worthy projects from all around the world to the attention of busy Christian laymen who would like to invest some time and money for the Lord. Perhaps the noblest description for such a project is, "Helping people to help themselves."

Essential tasks on many mission fields are being accomplished by people beyond the retirement age. Several of the happiest couples we have ever known have served or are serving in foreign lands — Mexico, Papua New Guinea, Ecuador, West Pakistan — capably handling tasks which free missionaries to perform the work they were trained and sent to do. In this day and age one does not necessarily have to be young to be useful on a mission field. We know one couple over eighty years of age who are having a great time working every day just as if they were young and assigned permanently. They feel needed because they are efficiently filling an essential spot. We have another friend who worked from her girlhood days in the U.S. Army Finance Center in St. Louis and then in Indianapolis, until retirement. All her life she had had a desire to go to the mission field. So after she retired, she spent three rewarding years working in Wycliffe's Mexico Branch headquarters in Tlalpan, mostly in the Finance Office. Jobs like this are available to the qualified seeker.

* * * * * * *

As I have been sitting here this evening, and the stories of these past events have passed swiftly through my mind, I cannot help wondering if this victorious achievement means that Otomi potential has reached its peak. I think not. I shall be very much surprised if their best days are not ahead. I believe every inch of this building will be in use every day. Not only will it benefit the people on Colony Hill and those within walking distance, but it will relieve pressures brought on by the influx of fiesta and special-occasion audiences. And there is still another use which I predict it will serve.

Almost as soon as we acquired the Honey land, Venancio shared with me a longtime dream of his. He felt the urgent need of an Otomi school. He dreamed of being able some day to found, build, and operate a Bible and vocational school for young Otomi. In the field known as La Vina adjoining Chapultepec was a knoll next to the El Maye road, very close to the town limits of Ixmiquilpan. This knoll perhaps covered an area containing slightly more than half an acre. Venancio had his eye on that knoll and called it the "hard ground." This he said was the logical site on which to build the Bible school. I became interested in his dream and joined in with his plans. Realizing that his vision could not become a reality until their farming enterprise became profitable, I committed resources to help make his dream come true.

I said to him, "I think you are entirely right in your idea of starting a Bible school, and I like the idea of making it a vocational school as well. I am with you all the way. You spearhead the idea to your people and encourage them to save their money toward building the school on the hard ground. It seems to me a perfect location. When you have enough money to start it, I will match the amount — peso for peso — to its completion." Actually, it appeared to be the best idea all of us had come up with since our relationship started. It was feasible and seemed to be God's plan. But for the next year or two, it took nearly all the brothers' profits to get their farming enterprise started and expanded, so that savings for a Bible school just were not possible.

All the time, however, the local Colony church continued to grow in such numbers as to exhaust all its facilities. By 1968 the Christians realized that they must have a new church. Within the next year or so, they showed us a building site they had chosen about four blocks south of the present new church, where they planned to construct a building seating some 2000 people. I never knew why, but it didn't materialize. The Bible school apparently got sidetracked in favor of a new church, and plans for that church were evidently abandoned in favor of this new church, Templo Sinai, whose dedication we are now attending. Everyone agrees that this is a God-given building, so perhaps the Lord wished that the giving and dedication of the New Testament should have priority, as it did in April, 1971.

The particular use I have predicted for this spacious Otomi church is that the Bible school Venancio has so long desired will be held here. The church, at least for the present, will doubtless be a much better place to hold the small classes that are presently scattered here and there in homes. In Templo Sinai, the balcony alone now holds 600 people, four times the capacity of the old former church in the Colony. The brethren designed and built this spacious, reinforced balcony with their own ingenuity and labor. It can safely be used to accommodate a capacity crowd, and can easily be partitioned into a number of classrooms. Along with numerous classrooms downstairs, it will furnish adequate facilities for a large Bible school for years to come.

From a business standpoint, it looks as if the church facilities will be more satisfactory and less expensive than if it was separately built on the hard ground of La Vina. However, I can see that perhaps La Vina would be a more appropriate spot on which to locate the vocational school. If and when they can afford to start work on it, my proposition still stands, to match peso for peso in the cost of its construction, if the Lord sees fit to spare my life until then. Not all young Otomi wish to become farmers, and one can see why Venancio feels the need to establish a vocational school to teach them profitable trades among their own people, rather than losing them in the throngs of the large cities. The school may become a reality sooner than we think.

Of prime importance, and most urgent at once, is an intensive campaign, properly coordinated throughout the Mezquital, to put to use the magnificent Otomi New Testament in every believer's home. That means literate Otomi, reading in the Otomi language. Where better can it start than from every pulpit? Knowing that Venancio believes that with all his heart, I presume he will urge every pastor under his leadership to take part in crash literacy courses by enrolling and attending classes where they study, learn to read, understand, and preach the Gospel from the Otomi Scriptures to every congregation. That probably will be the first and most important course offered in their new Bible school. Pastors should also teach their congregations elementary hygiene, sanitation, principles of improved diet, child care, good manners, and daily devotions. Some of these might be elective courses. I believe that within a year this church will become a beehive of activity.

I think it will also become a showcase, demonstrating to people who will come from far and near what happens when a people put their faith and trust in God and their shoulder to the wheel. I have heard men pray that their church would become a lighthouse on a hill — this one has become that and more. I see Templo Sinai as a revolving beacon, illuminating a whole dark valley that was once held in the clutches of witchcraft and superstition.

Before too many years, I believe it will outgrow its space and facilities. If it keeps up its present rate of growth, the leaders will again be pondering what to do with so many people. They will not give up in despair, however, but will rise to the challenge. It will not surprise me to hear that another church such as this is being built up north at Zimapan or even as far north as Tamazunchale in Huastecan country which overlaps Otomi land. Venancio will never lower his horizons, and I believe that some day I shall see missionaries sent out from this church in all four directions from the Mezquital Valley.

131

Have you heard any good news issuing from secular sources recently? Bad news is plentiful, but one "for sure" encouraging report is coming from worldwide missions. Enthusiasm for pioneer missions is contagious. I am glad that we were exposed and caught it.

By the way, if you ever attend Templo Sinai, as soon as the service is dismissed and you wish to shake hands and congratulate my Otomi pastor at the door, gently touch the palms of your fingers to his fingers. Do not grab his hand and work his arm up and down like a pump handle. That is the way I did at first, before I learned that it isn't polite.